BASALT REGIONAL LIBRARY DISTRICT

99 Midland Avenue
Basalt CO 81621
927-4311

DATE DUE

			4/23
GAYLORD			PRINTED IN U.S.A.

New Hampshire

New Hampshire

R. Conrad Stein

Children's Press®
A Division of Grolier Publishing
New York   London   Hong Kong   Sydney
Danbury, Connecticut

Frontispiece: Franconia Notch

Front cover: Aerial view of Hollis

Back cover: Blair Covered Bridge, Campton

Consultant: William Copley, Tuck Library, New Hampshire Historical Society

Please note: All statistics are as up-to-date as possible at the time of publication.

Visit Children's Press on the Internet at http://publishing.grolier.com

Book production by Editorial Directions, Inc.

Library of Congress Cataloging-in-Publication Data

Stein, R. Conrad.
   New Hampshire / R. Conrad Stein.
      144 p. 24 cm. — (America the beautiful. Second series)
   Includes bibliographical references and index.
   Summary : Introduces the geography, plants and animals, history, economy, language,
     religions, culture, and people of the state of New Hampshire.
   ISBN 0-516-21071-8
   1. New Hampshire—Juvenile literature. [1. New Hampshire.] I. Title. II. Series.
F34.3 .S74 2000
974.2—dc21   99-086345
                                                            CIP
                                                            AC

Acknowledgments

The author wishes to thank the New Hampshire Office of Travel and Tourism Development in Concord for assistance in preparing this book. Thanks also to the wonderful and friendly people of New Hampshire.

The White Mountains

Waterfall on
Pemigenasset River

Portsmouth Lighthouse

A statue of
John Stark

Contents

Rock climbing

Manchester

Biking on Great Glen Trails

Maple syrup

CHAPTER ONE

The Old Man of the Mountain

n the wildly beautiful White Mountains of New Hampshire rises a cliff with an unusual natural formation. Look at it from below and the cliff resembles the face of an old man. Some say the stone face looks cranky, that of a crusty old fellow who is easily annoyed. But New Hampshirites claim he is simply independent and shows his independence in firm facial features. The Old Man of the Mountain is New Hampshire's official state symbol. Drive New Hampshire roads and you will see his craggy face on highway signs. And you will be reminded that independence and the freedom to be different are valued in this state.

New Hampshire is one of only two states in the nation that has no income tax and no sales tax. The state motto reads "Live Free or Die," which sounds more like a commandment issued from the heavens than a motto. Its house of representatives has 400 members, twice as many as most states. Despite its differences, New Hampshire is clearly doing something right. In 1997, only 7.7 percent of its residents lived below the poverty level, the lowest

**Opposite: The Old Man
of the Mountain**

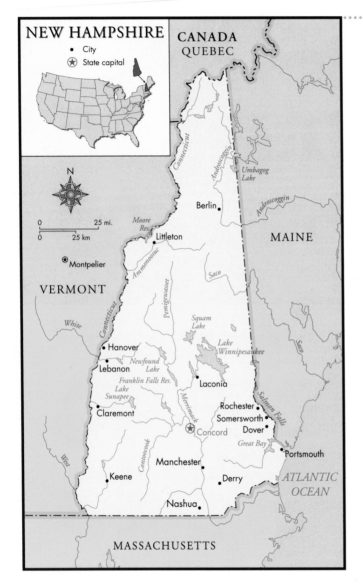

NEW HAMPSHIRE
- • City
- ⊛ State capital

CANADA
QUEBEC

Umbagog Lake

Berlin

Androscoggin

MAINE

Moore Res.

Littleton

Montpelier

Saco

Ammonoosuc

VERMONT

Pemigewasset

Squam Lake

White

Connecticut

Lake Winnipesaukee

Hanover

Newfound Lake

Lebanon

Franklin Falls Res.

Lake Sunapee

Laconia

Merrimack

Salmon Falls

Claremont

Rochester

Somersworth

Concord

Dover

Great Bay

Contoocook

Manchester

Portsmouth

West

Keene

Derry

ATLANTIC OCEAN

Nashua

MASSACHUSETTS

Geopolitical map of New Hampshire

such figure in the fifty states. It is third in the nation in terms of fewest crimes reported, and its public school system ranks as one of the best.

Tiny New Hampshire is forty-fourth in size among the states. With an estimated 1,185,000 people in 1998, it holds less than 1 percent of the nation's population. It is, however, a place of astonishing natural beauty, and this is one reason the state is growing so fast. In the past three decades, its population has increased by 75 percent.

New Hampshire is one of six states that make up the region called New England. Other New England states are Connecticut, Maine, Massachusetts, Rhode Island, and Vermont. New England is a beautiful and historic section of the eastern United States, known for its old churches and villages, its quaint covered bridges, and the blaze of colors that transform its trees in the fall.

New Englanders were once called Yankees, or Yanks for short. A typical Yankee was described as being very sharp in business dealings, frugal, and possessing a wry sense of humor. A story says a stranger once asked a New Hampshire apple farmer if he had lived on his farm all his life. The farmer thought about the question

The Portsmouth Lighthouse along New Hampshire's short coastline

and, in Yankee fashion, answered, "Not yet." Another heralded talent of New Englanders was "Yankee ingenuity," the ability to make something out of nothing. This sort of inventiveness has long driven the New Hampshire economy. New Hampshire has relatively poor farmland and few natural resources. Still, largely because of high-tech industries and an educated population, it is a prosperous state.

As one of the thirteen original English colonies, New Hampshire is older than the United States itself. It lies along the Atlantic seaboard, but its coastline is only 18 miles (29 kilometers) long. Concord is New Hampshire's capital and Manchester is its largest city. New Hampshire is nicknamed the Granite State because granite is the bedrock of its mountains. As you travel in New Hampshire, think of the Old Man of the Mountain who has had that same stony glint in his eye for hundreds of years. That old man is very much like the state—independent and different from the norm. And he is proud to be that way.

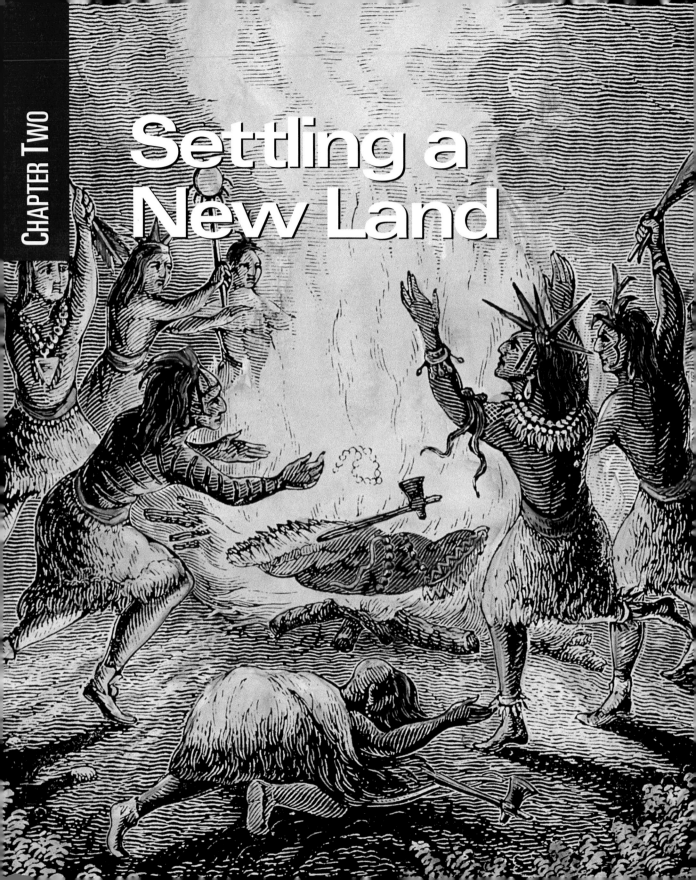

CHAPTER TWO

Settling a New Land

Thousands of years ago, bands of men and women from Asia crossed icy land bridges over the Bering Strait in what is now Alaska and began an amazing migration into another continent. Those first Americans were hunters who moved about the land spearing animals for meat. Eventually, they entered what is now the New England region and trekked across the land that would one day be the state of New Hampshire.

Native American stone tools found in New Hampshire

The First New Hampshirites

Little is known about the earliest settlers of New Hampshire. No doubt they found it an abundant land. The New Hampshire forests at that time were alive with deer, and the streams overflowed with huge bass and pike. Spear points, axes, and stone knives used by the first arrivals have been uncovered near Lake Winnipesaukee and along the Merrimack River near present-day Manchester.

About 3,000 years ago, the ancient people of this region learned to grow corn and squash. Agriculture allowed them to live in settled villages. They acquired skills such as pottery making and wood carving. Hunters and traders cut well-established paths through the forests. Centuries later, those paths were used by the first white settlers.

Opposite: A Native American ceremony

America's Stonehenge, a Mystery in History

At North Salem, New Hampshire, stands a stone structure that baffles archaeologists—men and women who study ancient peoples. It is called America's Stonehenge because it resembles the famous Stonehenge in England, a circular monument erected thousands of years ago. Who built America's Stonehenge? Why and when did they do it? Fierce arguments rage over this question. The New Hampshire structure is made up of stone blocks, some of which weigh ten tons. Tools found near the site are believed to be 4,000 years old, but it is not certain if the builders used those tools. Like England's Stonehenge, the building can be used to determine solar or lunar events. Some archaeologists speculate that Europeans who arrived centuries before Columbus put up the structure. Every day hundreds of people visit this curious ruin that sits on top of a rise appropriately named Mystery Hill. ■

Native American women gathering rice

It is estimated that some 5,000 Native Americans lived in New Hampshire when the first whites arrived. Most were members of the Algonquin-speaking family of Indians called the Abenaki. Their villages consisted of wigwams that were made of poles covered with animal hides and tree bark. The people moved often, and wigwams were easy to set up and dismantle. Corn was their staple food. Distant tribes often got together to trade goods and to indulge in music and dancing. A religious people, the New Hampshire Indians believed in an all-powerful creator and a host of lesser gods and spirits.

Historic Canoe

New Hampshire's Native Americans were aggressive traders. They built sturdy canoes and paddled many miles through rivers and lakes. One well-preserved canoe, found buried in the mud along a riverbank, was probably used by the Abenaki in the 1500s. The canoe, carved out of a single log, is now displayed at the Museum of New Hampshire History in Concord. ■

It is difficult to imagine what the Indians thought when they saw the first European ships along New Hampshire's Atlantic coast. Surely they were astounded. None had ever seen vessels so large, with sails towering like clouds above their decks. Yet many were unafraid. Reports claim that American Indians often paddled canoes out to meet the ships because they were eager to trade goods with the newcomers. But could any Indian who lived along the East Coast have even guessed what profound changes these strangers would bring to the land?

The Indian Mortar Stone

In the town of Franklin, a historical marker put up by the state points out the Indian Mortar Stone. It is a partially hollowed-out boulder that was used as a grinding stone by Abenaki people. The Abenaki put corn kernels on this mortar stone and ground the kernels to flour with another stone. White settlers, learning from the Indians, also ground their corn on this very stone. ■

Explorers and Settlers

Who was the first European to visit New Hampshire? According to written records, that honor goes to the English sea captain Martin Pring who took his sailing ship a few miles up the Piscataqua River and may have landed in Portsmouth in 1603. Along the banks of the river he wrote that he saw, "woods and sundry sorts of beasts, but no people." Two years later, the French explorer Samuel de Champlain landed on the New Hampshire coast.

In 1614, the Englishman John Smith arrived in New Hampshire. Earlier, Captain John Smith had established the first permanent English colony in the New World at Jamestown, Virginia. Smith was an idealist and believed this new land would welcome English settlers who sought freedom and independence. He wrote, "Here should be no landlords to rack us with high rents. . . . Here every man may be master of his own labor and land in a short time." It was Smith who suggested that the land north of Virginia should be called New England.

Unwittingly, the first European traders and fishermen who came to New England brought with them diseases that decimated the Indian population. From 1616 to 1619, a terrible epidemic of either measles or scarlet fever swept the Atlantic Coast. Europeans had lived with these sicknesses for many generations and had developed immunities to them, but the Native Americans had no such immunities. Some historians estimate that as many as nine of every ten Native Americans along the Atlantic Coast died during the great plague.

In November 1620, an overcrowded sailing ship struggled up the New England shore to present-day Massachusetts, and 102 exhausted and near-starving people climbed ashore. The ship was the *Mayflower*, and its passengers were the Pilgrims.

Just three years after the Pilgrims landed at Plymouth Rock, a group of hardy English people established a settlement in present-

John Smith came to New Hampshire in 1614.

The Indian Noah

In the 1600s, an Englishman named John Josselyn traveled around what is now New Hampshire and spoke to many local Indians. A chief told him a tribal legend that had been passed down among his people for many generations. The legend sounded amazingly like the story of Noah in the Bible. Here is Josselyn's rendition of the legend complete with English spellings and capitalizations in use at the time: "A great while agon their country was drowned, and all the People and other Creatures in it. Only one [man] and his [family], foreseeing the Floud, fled to the white mountains taking a hare along with them and so escaped; after a while the man sent the hare away. [When the hare did not return the people went down from the white mountains] and they lived many years, and had many Children, from which the Countrie was filled again with Indians." ■

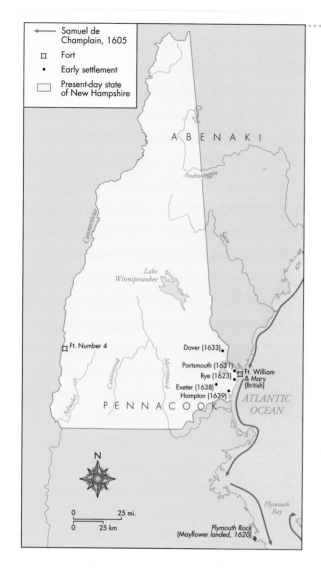

**Exploration of
New Hampshire**

day New Hampshire. In 1623, David Thomson, along with his wife and a handful of followers, built crude huts at what is now the town of Rye. Another settlement, headed by Edward Hilton, was founded at Dover at about the same time. The New Hampshire colonies were intended to be fishing villages and fur-trading outposts.

Principal sponsors for New Hampshire settlements were John Mason and Sir Ferdinando Gorges. The English government gave both men large tracts of land in present-day New Hampshire and Maine. It was Mason who named his holdings New Hampshire, after Hampshire, his native county in England. Ironically, Mason never saw New Hampshire. He died before he could visit the land he named.

The New Hampshire colonies achieved modest success. In the first thirty years of settlement, New Hampshire held some 1,000 English colonists. Four villages were established: Portsmouth (officially founded in 1631), Dover (1633), Exeter (1638), and Hampton (1639). Each of these villages was near the sea. The interior of New Hampshire was explored but not settled.

For much of the 1600s, New Hampshire was considered part of the larger colony of Massachusetts, but there were vast differences between the two English settlements. The Puritans who governed Massachusetts imposed strict religious laws on the people.

Sir Ferdinando Gorges
and John Mason
naming their provinces

New Hampshire enjoyed greater religious freedom, but also had periods of terrible religious intolerance. In 1660, a colonist named William Leddra was hanged for the crime of "being a Quaker." Two years later, a woman named Anna Coleman was tied to a post and whipped on her bare back. Her crime? Anna Coleman was also a Quaker. Though the Quakers were a gentle people, they were looked upon as a threat to the Puritan Church that ruled Massachusetts. Ultimately, religious freedom prevailed in colonial New Hampshire. By the early 1700s, one-third of the people of Dover were members of the Quaker Church.

Initially the Indians and the English lived in relative peace. The Indians coveted the goods the whites brought—iron pots and knives, fishhooks, axes, and other useful tools. Eagerly, they traded fur pelts for these marvelous items from afar. From the Indians, the settlers learned to cultivate corn, a crop unfamiliar to them. The

New Hampshire's Only Witch

The religious folk of Massachusetts lived in fear of witchcraft. This fear reached its peak in 1692 when twenty men and women were executed in Salem, Massachusetts, on the charge that they were witches. New Hampshire had only one major encounter with the witchcraft mania, however. In 1656, a neighbor woman accused Goodwife Walford of being a witch. The neighbor said in court that the two argued, and then, "She left me, and I was struck as with a clap of fire on the back, and [Goodwife Walford] vanished toward the waterside in the shape of a cat." Such an accusation could mean deep trouble in Puritan Massachusetts, but a New Hampshire court dismissed the charges against Goodwife Walford. In fact, Mrs. Walford was awarded money to be paid as damages by the neighbor who called her a witch. ■

Passaconaway was an Abenaki chief who was known as a religious mystic.

Indians also taught the English to build canoes, to make snowshoes, and to tap maple trees for sap to make into sugar.

An Abenaki chief named Passaconaway became a special friend of the whites, and he worked to preserve peace between his people and the colonists. Passaconaway was famed as a religious mystic who could, according to legends, "make the water burn, the rocks move, and the trees dance." It was said that when he died Passaconaway was drawn up New Hampshire's Mount Washington on a sled pulled by wolves.

The peace between the English and the Indians did not last. By the late 1600s, much of New Hampshire was a battleground. Fighting between the two peoples was made worse by a series of wars between France and England that spilled over to North America. Fear of Indian attack became part of the rigors of colonial life in New Hampshire.

The New Hampshire Colony Grows Up

In 1679, the English government declared New Hampshire to be a royal province. Now, New Hampshire was a separate colony, no longer a part of Massachusetts. John Cutt of Portsmouth was appointed New Hampshire's first governor. Although New Hampshire was an official colony, it had no set borders. For a time, New Hampshire had claims on the land that eventually became its neighbor state, Vermont. Indefinite borders discouraged settlement because people were reluctant to purchase land not knowing what colony they would be living in. As a result, in 1732, more than 100 years after settlement began, the population of New Hampshire stood at only about 12,500.

The greatest drawback to settlement was the Indian wars that rocked New Hampshire and all of New England in the late 1600s. The Native Americans of New England resented the colonists for pushing them off land they had held for generations. France, England's ancient rival, exploited this resentment to further their own interests. The French, too, had claims in North America, and they

The French and Indian Wars

For almost 100 years, France and England battled in North America, sweeping American Indians into their fury. Four major wars were fought. Today, the conflicts confuse students of history because they were collectively called the French and Indian Wars (plural), and the last one was called the French and Indian War (singular). All four were extensions of European wars. The four wars were: King William's War (1689–1697); Queen Anne's War (1702–1713); King George's War (1744–1748); the French and Indian War (1754–1763). ■

wanted to expel English settlers. French agents gave guns to their Indian allies and urged them to attack the British. The result was a series of deadly clashes that are known to history as the French and Indian Wars.

In periods between the wars, more settlers arrived in colonial New Hampshire. Between 1732 and 1742, the population doubled, reaching 24,000. Men and women from Britain established villages and named them after towns in their old country: Albany, Bristol, Winchester, Windsor. The fertile Connecticut River valley attracted

Fort Number 4

A living history of the French and Indian Wars is presented at Fort Number 4 just north of Charlestown. A stockade, called simply Fort Number 4, was built here in 1744. At one time, the fort withstood an attack by 400 French soldiers. Today, a replica of the old fort stands complete with high walls and a watchtower. Volunteers dressed in colonial costumes demonstrate seventeenth-century skills such as candle making and cooking over open fires. ■

farmers. Scotch-Irish pioneers established the town of Londonderry in 1719, and brought with them a new crop—the potato. The city of Rochester was founded in 1722; Concord in 1727; and Manchester in 1751. The colony's economy blended agriculture with industry. The making of linen—an industry that would eventually dominate the state—grew steadily during the colonial period. Lumber became the colony's most important product as tall straight trees from the New Hampshire woods furnished masts for hundreds of ships.

When they were not fighting the French or the Indians, the colonists enjoyed a peaceful lifestyle. For 120 years, not one public

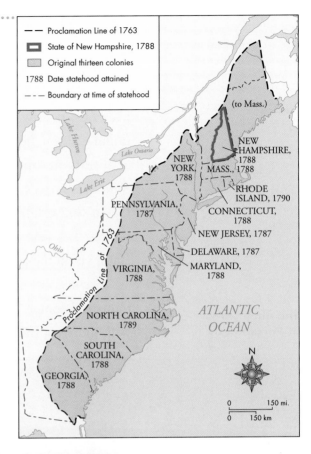

Historical map of the thirteen colonies

The lumber industry was important to New Hampshire's shipbuilding business.

execution took place in New Hampshire—at a time when stealing a pig could mean the death penalty. Religion dominated the social life of the colony. Most colonists were members of the Congregational Church, but more and more Quakers moved up from Massachusetts to enjoy the religious freedom of New Hampshire. Sunday services were the highlight of the week. The Reverend David Sutherland of the tiny town of Bath (founded in 1761) wrote, "For years we have had no stoves in the meeting-house of Bath; yet in the coldest weather, the house was always full."

The seaport city of Portsmouth was the colony's cultural and industrial center. Shipyards at Portsmouth built vessels that traded with the West Indies far to the south. Sea captains who grew rich

The navy yards at Portsmouth

The Richard Jackson House

New Hampshire's oldest house is in Portsmouth and dates back to 1664. It was once the home of a wealthy shipbuilder named Richard Jackson. It has been lovingly restored by the Society for the Preservation of New England Antiquities. Today, you may visit the Richard Jackson House in Portsmouth and enjoy its proud history. Many other historic houses are nearby. ■

on the West Indies trade built mansions on Portsmouth's main streets. The colony's first newspaper, the *New Hampshire Gazette*, was printed in Portsmouth in 1756. In 1761, a stagecoach line linked Portsmouth with Boston. For many years, Portsmouth was the New Hampshire colony's capital and seat of government.

The Wentworths of Portsmouth were the colony's most prominent family in the 1700s. John Wentworth served as lieutenant governor until his death in 1730. His son Benning was royal governor from 1741 to 1767. During Benning's term, seventy-five new towns were incorporated and the colony's population increased to 52,000. John Wentworth II, Benning's nephew, was governor from 1767 to 1775. He persuaded England's Earl of Dartmouth to donate 40,000 acres (16,200 hectares) of land to fund a school called Dartmouth College. Today, Dartmouth College (founded in 1770 in Hanover) is New Hampshire's most prestigious place of higher learning.

Dartmouth College was founded in 1770.

Even as a colony, New Hampshire displayed the fiery independence that would later characterize its personality. In 1774, as hatred of the British government grew in the colonies, a group of 400 New Hampshire men stormed the British-held Fort William and Mary that stood in the town of New Castle. The men quickly overwhelmed the fort, seizing guns, a cannon, and several barrels of gunpowder. These munitions were later used against the British army at the Battle of Bunker Hill. Storming the fort was the first military act of the American Revolution, and New Hampshirites who longed for independence led it.

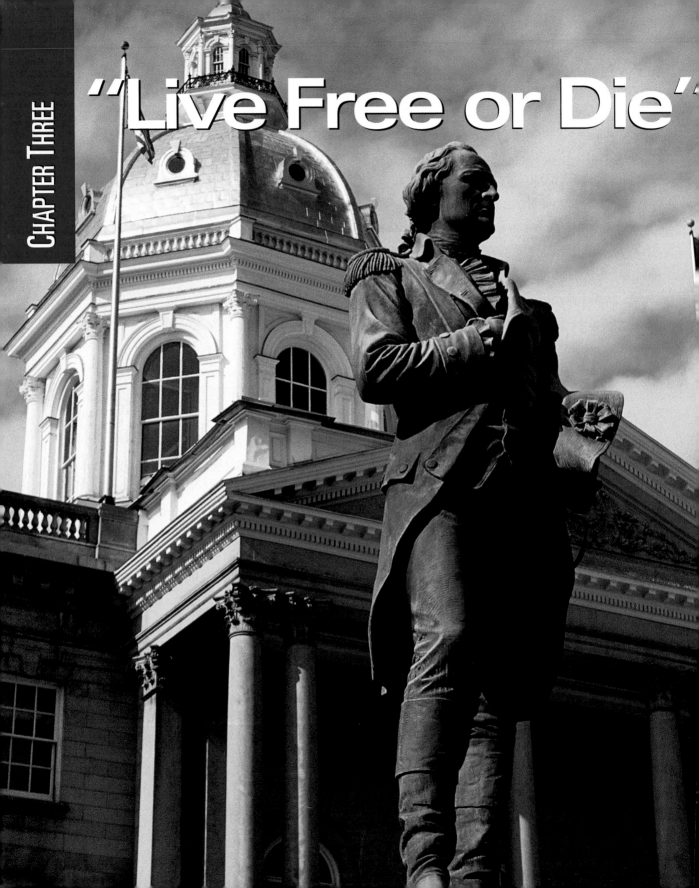

CHAPTER THREE

"Live Free or Die"

John Paul Jones hoisting the American flag above the *Ranger*

The French and Indian War (1754–1763) was costly—both in human life and in money. The war was won by Great Britain, but it drained the British treasury. To recover its losses, the British government decided to tax its thirteen colonies in America. The colonists argued that such measures as the tax on stamps (1765) and the tax on tea (1767) were illegal because the colonists had no representatives in the British Parliament. The slogan "Taxation without Representation Is Tyranny" echoed throughout the colonies. Outrage against taxes led to revolution. In April 1775, shots were fired at Lexington and Concord in Massachusetts, and the colonies went to war with Britain.

New Hampshire and Independence

New Hampshire was better prepared for war than were most other colonies. Ironically, Benning Wentworth (1737–1820), the colony's last royal governor, had made the preparations. Fearing renewal of

Opposite: A statue of John Stark at the New Hampshire state house

the French and Indian Wars, Wentworth insisted that New Hampshire keep three militia regiments on hand to fight all enemies of the British Crown. When the colonists turned against Great Britain, Wentworth was forced to flee from New Hampshire. His three regiments remained to fight for George Washington and the new United States of America.

New Hampshire men made up the majority of the troops in the Battle of Bunker Hill, fought near Boston on June 17, 1775.

Strawbery Banke

Strawbery Banke, so named because settlers in the 1630s used to pick wild berries here, is a neighborhood of lovely restored houses in Portsmouth, some of which are close to 300 years old. Prominent among the Strawbery Banke houses is the 1758 dwelling where John Paul Jones once lived (above). Jones is called the Father of the American navy. When a British warship demanded that he surrender his vessel, Jones shouted out, "I have not yet begun to fight." You may visit the Jones house where guides dressed as eighteenth-century sailors will tell you about the house and its famous resident. Step aboard! ■

The opposing British commander, General Thomas Gage, was impressed by the fighting qualities of the Bunker Hill defenders. Gage wrote, "They [the American forces] are now spirited up by a rage and enthusiasm as great as ever a people were possessed of." Despite early victories scored by the United States, the Revolutionary War dragged on for eight years, causing great suffering in the new nation.

Approximately 18,000 New Hampshire men enlisted in the war against the British. Hundreds more served as privateers who raided British ships off the New England coast. The Portsmouth shipyards built three large warships for the American navy: the

John Stark, New Hampshire's greatest war hero

Raleigh, the *America*, and the *Ranger*. The *Ranger*, which was commanded by the famous seaman John Paul Jones (1747–1792), was the first warship of any kind to carry an American flag.

New Hampshire's greatest Revolutionary War hero was John Stark (1728–1822), who was born in the town of Londonderry. Stark led a mostly New Hampshire force to victory in a battle at Bennington in present-day Vermont. The 1777 Battle of Bennington thwarted a British plan to cut the northern colonies in half. Although its men were deeply involved in the struggle, New Hampshire was the only one of the thirteen colonies that saw no battles fought on its land.

Even while fighting raged, the former

colonies worked to proclaim their independence and to form a new government. Three New Hampshire men signed the Declaration of Independence on July 4, 1776, announcing to the world that the thirteen colonies were now an independent nation. In January 1776, New Hampshire was the first of the original colonies to have its own constitution. Then, in June 1788, New Hampshire became the ninth state to ratify the U.S. Constitution.

A New State and a New Nation

At war's end, political power in New Hampshire still rested in the cities near the sea, principally Portsmouth and Exeter. But the land along the Merrimack and Connecticut Rivers lured farmers, and many settled in the western part of the state. In 1781, pioneers in the region triggered a crisis when thirty-six towns broke away from New Hampshire and temporarily joined Vermont. Citizens in those western towns claimed that state politicians based in Portsmouth were ignoring them. It took the persuasive power of General George Washington to convince the towns to stay in the New Hampshire fold.

Josiah Bartlett

Josiah Bartlett (1725–1795) of New Hampshire was one of fifty-six members of the Continental Congress who signed the Declaration of Independence. Bartlett lived for many years in the New Hampshire village of Kingston, where he practiced medicine. He was one of the first doctors to treat malaria with the drug quinine. He served as New Hampshire's governor from 1790 to 1794. The town of Bartlett, today a popular winter resort in the White Mountains, was named after this New Hampshire statesman. ■

The Mt. Kearsarge Indian Museum

By 1750, the Abenaki Indians had virtually disappeared from the state. Many had moved west or gone to Canada and many others were killed by war and disease. But Native American culture lives on at the Mount Kearsarge Indian Museum in the town of Warner. Enter the museum and begin a journey through Native American history. Guides show guests how the Indian peoples treated disease with herbs, made baskets and canoes, and celebrated with music and dance. ■

Concord was made the state capital in 1808.

The 1800 census shows that New Hampshire had a population of 183,858. Many of the farmers and merchants had moved to New Hampshire from Massachusetts. For almost a century, Portsmouth served as the capital of the colony. But with the bulk of the people now living to the west, New Hampshire leaders sought a new capital city. In 1808, the state legislature made Concord the capital. Concord, which sits on the banks of the Merrimack River, was in the center of the state's most populous region.

Agriculture was the mainstay of New Hampshire's economy. In 1800, eight of every ten

Uncle Sam

In 1812, the United States fought a second war with Great Britain. For New Hampshire and the nation, the War of 1812 provided an enduring symbol. A merchant named Samuel Wilson of New Hampshire provided U.S. forces with beef. His family called him Uncle Sam, and Wilson used the initials "U.S." to identify his barrels of beef. Because the country and the uncle had the same initials, Americans began identifying Wilson as a superpatriot. Today, a historical marker in the town of Mason points out the cottage once owned by Samuel Wilson, otherwise known as Uncle Sam. ■

New Hampshirites worked the land. But the state's best farmland in the Connecticut and Merrimack River valleys quickly filled up. New farmers were forced to go into the hills where the land was rocky and too steep to be properly plowed. Because traditional crops such as corn, wheat, and hay were difficult to grow in the hill country, farmers there tried to raise sheep. Some were successful, but many hill farms failed.

In the early 1800s, however, industry blossomed in New Hampshire. A cotton mill was established in New Ipswich in 1804, and by 1810, the state had twelve cotton mills. Waterwheels built in many of New Hampshire's swift streams were used to run power equipment. A power loom at Manchester in 1819 began that city's manufacturing history. A shoe factory opened in Weare in 1823. New Hampshire's first railroad was completed between Nashua and Lowell, Massachusetts, in 1838. Four years later, railroad tracks were laid between Nashua and Concord. A seventy-four-gun warship, the *Washington*, was launched in 1815 at Portsmouth Naval Yards. Portsmouth later built many of the excit-

Wonderful Wagons

Concord Coaches were horse-drawn wagons made in Concord from 1827 to 1902. They became famous throughout the country. A typical Concord Coach could weigh more than a ton and sold for what was then the whopping price of $1,000. These rugged wagons could roll over rough roads without breaking down. Because of their durability, Concord Coaches were of vital importance in opening the American West. ■

ing clipper ships that raced from one world port to another at record-breaking speeds.

One of the great U.S. statesmen of the nineteenth century was Daniel Webster (1782–1852), who was born in Salisbury (now Franklin), New Hampshire. He attended Dartmouth College and practiced law in Portsmouth. Webster moved to Boston as a young man and soared to fame as a Massachusetts senator. A brilliant orator, Webster sought to ease bitter feelings between the Northern and Southern states over the issue of slavery. For years, schoolchildren in New England were required to memorize and recite lines from Webster's famous speeches: "Liberty *and* Union, now and forever, one and inseparable."

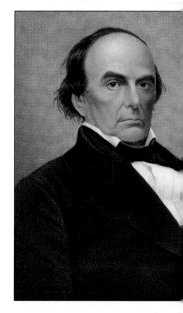

Daniel Webster was a famous orator from New Hampshire.

The only U.S. president to come from New Hampshire was Franklin Pierce (1804–1869). Born in Hillsborough in 1804, Pierce was from a political family. His father was New Hampshire's governor from 1827 to 1828 and again from 1829 to 1830. In 1837, New Hampshire sent Franklin Pierce to the U.S. Senate. He served as a general in the Mexican-American War (1846–1848), and was elected U.S. president in 1852. The explosive question of slavery dominated his administration. Pierce's time as president (1853–1857) was also complicated by the poor health of his wife, Jane Means Appleton Pierce. Mrs. Pierce hated Washington and longed to return to the family's home in New Hampshire.

The Civil War and the Rise of Industry

On April 12, 1861, Southern troops fired on Fort Sumter, a U.S. Army post in Charleston, South Carolina. The shots triggered the Civil War, which lasted for four terrible years.

Slavery was the main cause of the conflict, but it was not an issue in the Granite State. New Hampshire had outlawed slavery shortly after the Revolutionary War (1775–1783). By the mid-1800s, only a handful of African-Americans lived in the state. Yet New Hampshire was solidly behind Abraham Lincoln and the Northern cause. Almost 40,000 New Hampshire men served in the Civil War and some 4,700 died in the fighting. One regiment, the Fifth New Hampshire Volunteers, suffered a greater casualty rate than any other similar-sized unit in the Northern armies.

New Hampshire's growing industrial strength contributed to the North's final victory. Textile mills in the city of Troy produced

The Pierce Manse

The spirit of Franklin Pierce lives on in the Pierce Manse in Concord. It is officially called a *manse*, an old word meaning "family home." Built about 1844, it was once the home of the fourteenth president. Now open to tourists, the Pierce Manse is one of the most popular sites in Concord. ■

John Parker Hale

Born in Rochester, New Hampshire, John Parker Hale (1806–1873) practiced law and was elected to the U.S. Senate in 1846. In the Senate, he was an uncompromising abolitionist. John C. Calhoun, proslavery senator from South Carolina, once remarked, "[I] would sooner argue with a maniac from Bedlam than with the senator from New Hampshire on the question of Slavery." John Parker Hale's statue now stands on the lawn at the New Hampshire capitol. ■

rugged "New Hampshire blankets" that kept horses of the Northern cavalry warm. The Amoskeag textile mills in Manchester turned raw cotton into cloth and made thousands of uniforms for soldiers. The Amoskeag Manufacturing Company (named after a waterfall on the Merrimack River) also made railroad cars and train engines. Warships built at Portsmouth Naval Shipyard helped blockade Southern ports.

The Civil War ended in April 1865 with the North victorious. One of the final acts of the war came when the Thirteenth New Hampshire Regiment led a march on Richmond, Virginia, the Southern capital.

After the war, the state's farming communities declined. Many farmers who had struggled for years to make a living from the stubborn soil in the hill country finally gave up their quest. The farmers moved to the cities to take industrial jobs or left the state to try their luck elsewhere. From 1860 to 1870, New Hampshire's population declined from 326,073 to 318,300. That decade was the only ten-year period in the state's history that saw a population decrease.

Sugar River Mills in Newport

In the late 1800s, industry was the backbone of the state's economy. The Amoskeag Manufacturing Company in Manchester became the largest cotton mill in the world. Textile mills in Keene produced flannel shirts famous for their toughness. New Hampshire factories excelled at making boots and shoes. Logging remained a vital industry, and paper mills opened in the northern city of Berlin. The town of Rochester was transformed from a farming village into an industrial city making woolen goods, leather, and bricks. A company in Nashua became one of the nation's largest makers of wristwatches.

Often the shift from farms to factories was an unhappy experience for workers. Textile mills in New Hampshire and other states used unskilled people to operate looms and cut cloth. These companies were notorious for employing women and children and paying near-starvation wages. Millworkers in Manchester regularly

In the late 1800s, Manchester was becoming a large industrial city.

toiled sixteen hours a day. Women employees earned less than $2 a week. Children as young as ten got $1 a week. New Hampshire, however, soon passed laws prohibiting child labor and protecting the rights of workers. In many cases, New Hampshire's worker-protection laws were the first such measures enacted anywhere in America.

The industrial revolution sweeping New Hampshire changed the makeup of the population. Before the Civil War, more than 90 percent of New Hampshirites were Yankees whose ancestors came from Great Britain. Then factories lured workers from outside the state. Many of the new workers were European or Canadian immigrants. By 1890, almost 20 percent of the state's residents were foreign-born. French-Canadians were the largest foreign-born group. Other immigrants came from Poland, Italy, Scandinavia, Germany, Austria, Russia, Czechoslovakia, Greece, and Hungary. Manchester, the most industrialized of the state's cities, became a mixture of nationalities. It is estimated that forty ethnic groups speaking fifty different languages lived in Manchester during the late 1800s.

CHAPTER FOUR

Twentieth-Century New Hampshire

In 1900, New Hampshire's population was 411,588. During the previous 100 years, the state had reinvented itself by attracting industries and new people. Despite the changes, New Hampshire never lost its independence, and the people still insisted on doing things their own special way.

President Theodore Roosevelt (near center) led the negotiations between the Russians and the Japanese that resulted in the Treaty of Portsmouth.

Trials and Triumphs

In 1905, tiny New Hampshire captured world headlines when representatives from Japan, Russia, and the United States met in Portsmouth. The representatives signed final agreements to conclude the Russo-Japanese War, a conflict that involved hundreds of thousands of troops and dozens of warships. U.S. president Theodore Roosevelt had suggested Portsmouth as an ideal place to hold a peace conference. The result was the Treaty of Portsmouth,

Opposite: The Piscataqua River at Portsmouth

which made Japan a major power. President Roosevelt won the Nobel Peace Prize in 1906 for his efforts.

Sadly there was little peace in the world shortly after the Portsmouth Treaty. In 1914, Europe exploded into war and three years later, the United States joined the conflict. More than 20,000 New Hampshire men and women served in World War I. Of that number, 697 were killed and more than 100 were decorated for valor. Once again, New Hampshire's industries contributed to the war effort. Uniforms and army boots were made in Manchester and Nashua, while workers at the Portsmouth Navy Yards assembled the U.S. Navy's first submarine. World War I, which was called "the war to end all wars," ended in 1918.

The White Mountains National Forest

The White Mountains National Forest is the largest expanse of public land in New England. The forest covers 769,147 acres (311,505 ha) and it includes 1,267 miles (2,039 km) of hiking trails and forty-five lakes and ponds. Woodlands in the White Mountains cover almost 12 percent of the state and contain some of the most wildly beautiful scenery New Hampshire has to offer. But 100 years ago, this natural paradise seemed doomed.

For decades loggers had stripped much of the White Mountains bare of its trees, and devastating forest fires had turned vast tracts of woods into ashes. A sign at a White Mountains logging exhibit says of the late nineteenth century: "It was a time of large fortunes made and lost, a time of tree slaughter, and a time of fires unequaled before or since." Thanks largely to a courageous New Hampshire congressman named John Weeks (1860–1926), the great forest got a second chance at life. As a result of the Weeks Law, the federal government began buying White Mountain forest property, and today's national forest is the happy result. ■

The early 1900s was a time of progress for New Hampshire. Dams and hydroelectric generators were built on its rivers and the state government gave towns financial assistance to pave roads. A statewide board of education was formed with the aim of improving schools. The University of New Hampshire was created out of the old College of Agriculture and Mechanical Arts. The federal government acquired thousands of woodland acres in the White Mountains and proclaimed them a national forest.

By the 1920s, the textile plants centered in Manchester were aging. To compete with their rivals, many textile companies in New Hampshire cut workers' wages by 20 percent. In 1922, workers at Amoskeag Mills in Manchester went on strike over declining wages. It was a bitter strike that lasted nine months and caused severe suffering among the working people.

Amoskeag Mills in Manchester

Hard Times and War

In 1929, the stock market collapsed, launching the Great Depression of the 1930s. Banks failed and businesses closed. Around the country, one in four workers lost their jobs. Industrial states such as New Hampshire were the hardest hit. Wages in New Hampshire were reduced by more than 10 percent between 1929 and 1931. By 1934, the cruelest year of the Great Depression, thousands of New Hampshirites were unemployed.

A casualty of the Great Depression was the Amoskeag Mills in Manchester. In 1916, the Amoskeag Mills was in its prime— an industrial giant. The company's six-story factory buildings spread along both sides of the Merrimack River for more than 1 mile (1.6 km). Some 17,000 people—half of them women— worked at the mills. The company boasted that its 23,000 looms produced enough cloth every two months to place a band all the way around the world. But by 1936, the Amoskeag Mills was bankrupt. Reduced demand because of the depression was one cause of the mills' failure. Also during the 1930s, petticoats

New Hampshire and the CCC

At the height of the Great Depression, a federal government agency called the Civilian Conservation Corps (CCC) put unemployed young men to work on conservation projects. More than 20,000 CCC workers toiled in New Hampshire. The workers, many of them teenagers, cut hiking trails through woods, built forest-fire lookout towers, and cleared picnic areas. A tiny museum at Bear Brook State Park in Allenstown displays photographs and other items from the CCC experience of the 1930s. ■

The USS *Albacore*

Hundreds of visitors line up each day on the Portsmouth waterfront to tour the World War II submarine USS *Albacore*. The vessel, built in Portsmouth during the war years, is now permanently displayed in that city and enjoyed by young and old. ■

and long dresses were no longer fashionable, so there was less demand for fabric.

On a peaceful Sunday morning in December 1941, Japanese warplanes suddenly roared off the decks of aircraft carriers and bombed the U.S. Navy base in Pearl Harbor, Hawaii. President Franklin Roosevelt called December 7 "a date that will live in infamy." That shocking air raid catapulted the United States into World War II (1939–1945).

Almost 100,000 New Hampshire men and women served in that war. Once more, New Hampshire's factories hummed with activity, churning out war materials. The Portsmouth Naval Yards

The Stark Prisoner-of-War Camp

In early 1944, workers built a high fence and four watchtowers around a 1930s CCC camp and converted it into New Hampshire's only prisoner-of-war (POW) compound. About 250 German POWs lived there until 1946 when they were repatriated to Germany. Now and then, an aging German veteran returns to see the place where he spent several years of his youth. ■

became a major producer of submarines, while other New Hampshire factories made uniforms and boots for soldiers.

In July 1944, representatives of forty-four countries met at Bretton Woods in the town of Bartlett in the heart of the White Mountains. World War II was drawing to a close and the representatives hoped to repair wartime damage by simplifying the transfer of money between nations. Many discussions took place while the delegates walked amid the lovely mountain scenery. For that reason, the meeting has always been called the Bretton Woods Conference. It resulted in the creation of the International Monetary Fund.

New Hampshire, like the rest of the country, experienced a suburban explosion after World War II. By the 1950s, young families hungered for their own homes and patches of green yard. In New Hampshire, this led to dynamic growth in the southern half of the state. The population was further boosted as people from northern Massachusetts spilled over into southern New Hampshire. Soon critics complained that two New Hampshires were developing— one in the industrialized and fast-growing south, and another in the rather stagnant and largely rural northern half of the state.

The Wright Museum

World War II was a time of fear, frustration, and sadness. Yet there was a certain energy and spirit in the war years as the American people worked together for victory. The Wright Museum, situated on a 6-acre (2.4-ha) site in Wolfeboro, keeps that spirit alive with its collection of vehicles, films, music, and other memorabilia. The museum invites guests to step back in time and relive the 1940s when many Americans served on what was popularly called the home front. ■

Modern New Hampshire

New Hampshire helped launch the United States into the space age on May 5, 1961, when Alan B. Shepard Jr. (1923–1998) rocketed off Earth in a tiny capsule called *Freedom Seven*. Shepard, who was born in East Derry, was a navy test pilot before he joined the space program. His flight in *Freedom Seven* lasted only fifteen minutes, but it was the first time the United States had put a man into space. A month earlier, Russia had launched cosmonaut Yuri Gagarin into orbit, making him the first man in space. An intense competition developed between the two countries. Millions of Americans watched Shepard's flight on television, hoping it would restore leadership to the United States. In 1971, Alan Shepard commanded the Apollo 14 moon landing.

Alan Shepard led the Apollo 14 mission.

Traditionally, New Hampshirites dislike paying taxes. Yet everyone agrees that New Hampshire must pay for services such as highways and schools. To finance education, New Hampshire started a lottery in 1964 called the Sweepstakes. It was the first lottery sponsored by any state in more than sixty years. Many politicians around the country criticized the Sweepstakes, claiming it would lead people into deplorable gambling habits. But New

Sharon Christa McAuliffe

On January 28, 1986, seven smiling astronauts marched into the huge space shuttle *Challenger*. One of those astronauts was Sharon Christa McAuliffe (1948–1986). A history teacher at Concord High School, she was slated to be the first civilian in space. McAuliffe was chosen from 11,000 other teachers to rocket above Earth and then return and share her experiences with her students. Thousands of spectators watched the rocket carrying *Challenger* lift off from its launching pad. Seventy-two seconds later—in a flash of horror—the craft exploded. All seven crew members were killed.

A later investigation blamed a faulty rubber ring for the disaster.

Today, the Christa McAuliffe Planetarium stands in Concord, the city where she taught. It is an exciting museum where guests view the universe through a 40-foot (12-meter)-tall domed theater. Daily planetarium shows, children's workshops, and teachers' seminars are also part of the programming. The museum provides a thrilling way to learn about the universe. It is certain that Christa McAuliffe, an outstanding teacher, would be proud of the institution named in her honor. She once said, "I touch the future: I teach." ■

Hampshire stuck with the program. Today, most states have lotteries to help finance education.

The population of New Hampshire doubled between 1960 and 1988—jumping from 606,921 to 1,100,000. The state's Golden Triangle, a region from Manchester to Nashua to Portsmouth, became one of New England's most industrialized areas. Many of the new businesses moving into the Golden Triangle were high-tech firms that attracted educated men and women as workers. The once picturesque rural roads in Rockingham County, however, became lined with fast-food restaurants. In 1980, Governor Hugh J. Gallen complained, "I drive along some of the roads in southern New Hampshire and I can't see the signs

for the signs. This growth will destroy our quality of life if we don't do something about it."

The state's most passionate quality-of-life issue in recent memory involved the construction and operation of the Seabrook Nuclear Power Plant. In 1976, ground was broken to build this state-of-the-art nuclear generator at the town of Seabrook Beach, which lies along the ocean just 2 miles (3.2 km) from the Massachusetts border. Its backers boasted the plant would furnish 60 percent of New Hampshire's need for electric power. When construction began, engineers estimated Seabrook would cost $2 billion. Ten years later, the cost had soared to $6 billion, and the Seabrook Company went bankrupt.

SUN POWER
NO NUKES

UKES are
healthy
for
children and
other living
things

NUKES KILL
PLUG INTO THE SUN
PLYMOUTH, N.H.

**Protesters at the
Seabrook Nuclear
Power Plant**

Angry opponents of the Seabrook project claimed an accident at the nuclear generator could poison the surrounding air and kill untold numbers of people. People from Massachusetts and New Hampshire banded together in an organization called the Clamshell Alliance to resist building the facility. On May 1, 1977, about 1,400 protestors were arrested during a sit-in at the construction site—the largest mass arrest in New Hampshire's history. Despite the protests, however, the plant finally began operation in

August 1990. Seabrook was the last nuclear power plant built in the United States.

In the 1980s, New Hampshire generated more new jobs per capita than any other state. Then, however, the state and the nation slipped into a minirecession, and from 1989 to 1992, New Hampshire lost an estimated 50,000 jobs. But prosperity reigned again later in the decade. As the twenty-first century began, job prospects in New Hampshire were among the brightest in the fifty states. The population continued to rise as more and more people came to live in this lovely and prosperous state.

CHAPTER FIVE

Scenic Wonders

Follow a special trail in the Crawford Notch State Park. It's a tough hike, almost 1.5 miles (2.4 km) long and mostly uphill. Finally, you will see the Arethusa Falls, the highest waterfall in New Hampshire. It is a sight well worth the hike. Tired of hiking? Relax on the beach and enjoy a view of the Atlantic Ocean at Odiorne Point State Park. New Hampshire offers visitors an amazing variety of outdoor wonders. Forest-covered mountains, a windswept seacoast, pleasant farm country, beautiful lakes, and rushing rivers—all this wrapped up in one small but very surprising package.

Crawford Notch State Park

Geography and the Shape of the Land

New Hampshire resembles a wedge of pie cut unevenly at its left or western end. Its seacoast sits on the southeast corner. Above the coast, the Piscataqua and Salmon Falls Rivers make up part of the

Opposite: Autumn at Mount Washington

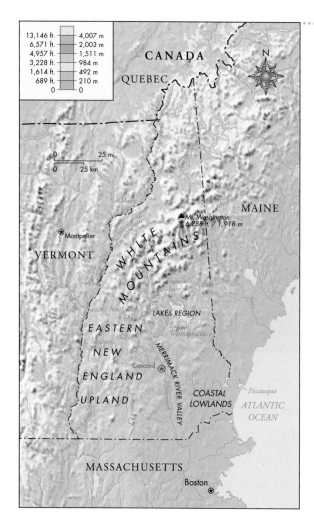

New Hampshire's topography

state's boundary with Maine. A man-made line stretches north to complete the Maine–New Hampshire border. In the far north, New Hampshire is separated from Quebec in Canada by Halls Stream, a branch of the Connecticut River. On the west, the Connecticut River makes up the border with Vermont. A man-made line separates New Hampshire from Massachusetts in the south.

New Hampshire covers 9,283 square miles (24,043 square kilometers) and ranks forty-fourth in size among the fifty states. Its greatest distance from north to south is 180 miles (290 km), and its greatest distance from east to west is 93 miles (150 km).

Geologists divide New Hampshire's land into three main regions: the White Mountains in the north, the Eastern New England Upland in the west and south, and the Coastal Lowlands in the southeast. These regions are determined by land features and the kinds of vegetation and animal life the land supports.

The Far North State

New Hampshire is not the most northern spot in the United States, but it is still "up there." Drive Highway 145 through the tiny town of Clarksville in northern New Hampshire and a state historical marker announces you have crossed the 45th parallel, which marks the halfway point between the equator and the North Pole. ∎

The towering White Mountains contain such breathtaking beauty they are often called "the Switzerland of America." Rising there are eighty-six mountain peaks, eight of which are more than 1 mile (1.6 km) high. The tallest mountain, and the highest point in New Hampshire, is Mount Washington at 6,288 feet (1,918 m). The peak of Mount Washington is often cloud-capped and has traces of snow late into the summer. Flanking Mount Washington is the Presidential Range whose individual peaks are named after various presidents: Monroe, Jefferson, Adams, Jackson, Madison, and others. At 5,798 feet (1,768 m), Mount Adams is the second- highest peak in the state.

The river valleys in the Eastern New England Upland region are the site of farms and industrialized cities. Three of New Hamp-

The White Mountains in snow

The Top of the Mount

On a clear day, you can stand on Mount Washington's peak and look out over five states—New Hampshire, Maine, Vermont, Massachusetts, and New York—and even into Canada. ■

shire's biggest cities—Manchester, Nashua, and Concord—are in the Merrimack River valley. Not all of New Hampshire's lofty peaks stand in the White Mountains. Mount Monadnock, 3,165 feet (965 m); Croydon Peak, 2,781 feet (848 m); and Mount Kearsarge, 2,937 feet (896 m) are all in the Eastern New England Upland region.

New Hampshire's seacoast, only 18 miles (29 km) long, is the smallest seacoast of any New England state except for landlocked Vermont. Most of the coast is public beach, making it a popular spot with tourists. Inland are historic villages reminding visitors that the English colonists settled the seacoast first.

The Isles of Shoals

The Isles of Shoals are a group of nine small islands lying 9 miles (14 km) off New Hampshire's coast. Five of the nine islands belong to Maine and four to New Hampshire. The Englishman John Smith discovered the islands in 1614. Legend says the notorious pirate Blackbeard buried treasure on one of them. Sailors claim they see ghosts at night near Babb's Cove. At one time, the islands held a sizable Norwegian fishing colony. Today about 100,000 visitors a year take boat trips to the Shoals to see the wonderful bird and marine life. ■

Rivers, Lakes, and Climate

The Granite State has more than 40,000 miles (64,360 km) of rivers and streams. Major rivers begin in the northern mountains and channel rain and melted snow to the southern valleys. So many rivers begin in New Hampshire that one of the state's official nicknames is the Mother of Rivers. The Connecticut River originates near New Hampshire's border with Canada and flows into Massachusetts. The Merrimack River takes water from the White Mountains and cuts through the center of the state on its southward course. The Androscoggin and Saco Rivers flow east and eventually enter Maine. The Piscataqua and its branches empty into the Atlantic Ocean.

The Connecticut River at the New Hampshire–Vermont border

Waterfalls

There are more than 100 waterfalls in the White Mountains region alone. Walk the Falling Waters Trail at Franconia Notch State Park and you'll see five falls of various heights. Beaver Falls State Park near Colebrook has one of the state's most scenic waterfalls. Champney Falls near Littleton is a scenic delight. ■

The Lost River

In 1852, a local man tripped while walking in the White Mountains. He disappeared under a boulder, fell 15 feet (4.6 m), and was surprised to find himself unharmed and standing hip-deep in water. The stream the man plunged into was called the Lost River because it is so difficult to see from Earth's surface. Today, tourists enjoy exploring the river and claim it isn't lost at all; it's merely playing hide-and-seek. ■

Nowhere in New Hampshire are you far from water. About 1,300 lakes are sprinkled around the state, covering nearly 20 percent of the region. The largest body of water is Lake Winnipesaukee in central New Hampshire. Lake Winnipesaukee spreads over 72 square miles (186 sq km), is ringed by 183 miles (294 km) of shoreline, and contains 274 major islands. Other large lakes are Ossipee, Newfound, Squam, Sunapee, and Winnisquam. In the far north are two large bodies of water with rather unimaginative names: First Connecticut Lake and Second Connecticut Lake. Waters from the Connecticut River feed both lakes.

The Lakes Region

Lake Winnipesaukee sits in the center of an area that state officials call the Lakes Region. Why the name? The reason is quite simple. The region has 273 lakes—large and small. ▪

The state's wealth of rivers and lakes attests that it has plenty of rainfall. Every year New Hampshire about 42 inches (107 centimeters) of precipitation, which includes rain and melted snow. Droughts are few, but floods can occur. Older people still talk about the terrible flood of 1936, the worst in state history, which left thousands of people homeless and closed factories. That flood struck during the Great Depression and added to the people's miseries.

Generally, New Hampshire enjoys a pleasant if somewhat cold climate. Summers are mild with low humidity. Winters are long and cold, but they delight lovers of winter sports. However, there is a thorn in this rosy picture. The weather in New Hampshire is changeable, and sometimes dangerously so. Major storms that burst out of the Great Lakes to the west can turn a fine summer day into a thundering gale. Some of the strongest winds ever recorded roared over Mount Washington in April 1934, when wind speeds reached 231 miles (372 km) per hour. The wide range of weather can be seen in the record temperatures measured in the state. The thermometer dipped to a low of –46°F (–43°C) at Pittsburg on January 28, 1925, and reached a high of 106°F (41°C) at Nashua on July 4, 1911.

Most New Hampshire residents are used to long, cold winters.

New Hampshire's Geographical Features

Total area; rank	9,283 sq. mi. (24,043 sq km); 44th
Land; rank	8,969 sq. mi. (23,230 sq km); 44th
Water; rank	314 sq. mi. (813 sq km); 46th
Inland water; **rank**	314 sq. mi. (813 sq km); 43rd
Geographic center	Belknap, 3 miles (5 km) east of Ashland
Highest point	Mount Washington, 6,288 feet (1,918 m)
Lowest point	Sea level along the Atlantic coast
Largest city	Manchester
Population; rank	1,113,915 (1990 census); 41st
Record high temperature	106°F (41°C) at Nashua on July 4, 1911
Record low temperature	–46°F (–43°C) at Pittsburg on January 28, 1925
Average July temperature	68°F (20°C)
Average January temperature	19°F (–7°C)
Average annual precipitation	42 inches (107 cm)

Gifts of Nature

Some 85 percent of New Hampshire is forest-land. Experts claim the forests support seventy-four species of trees. Generally these species grow in three zones. In the southeast part of the state, the white pine prevails. In the central section and the White Mountains stand hardwoods such as sugar maple, beech, and yellow birch. Red spruce, balsam fir, and tamarack dominate in the far north of the state. The red maple, the most common tree in New Hampshire, is found in all those zones. In the fall, the forests change from rich green to dazzling gold and orange.

Wildflowers, shrubs, and grasses thrive in New Hampshire. Meadows dotting the forest

A field of dandelions in the White Mountains

State Parks

Enjoy nature at its fullest in one of New Hampshire's state parks. New Hampshire has 42 state parks and 116 state forests. The largest of the state parks, with 13,000 acres (5,265 ha) of forest-land, is Pisgah State Park near Winchester. The sprawling White Mountains National Forest extends into Maine. ■

lands are ablaze with fireweed, wild asters, black-eyed Susans, daisies, and goldenrod. Common shrubs include elders, blueberries, mountain laurel, and sumacs. Rhododendron State Park near the town of Fitzwilliam thrills guests with 16 acres (6.5 ha) of wild rhododendrons.

In New Hampshire, it is possible to see a deer in your front yard even if you live in Concord, the state capital. A huge black bear will sometimes blunder onto the main street of a large town. The state's bear population has grown from an estimated 500 in 1900 to 3,000 today. Bears have moved into regions where they have not been seen in generations. Other common animals include beavers, chipmunks, muskrats, minks, porcupines, raccoons, red and gray squirrels, skunks, rabbits, and woodchucks. Coyotes and wolves are heard, but rarely seen, in the New Hampshire wilds.

Black bears are common in New Hampshire.

The Fells State Historic Site

In the nineteenth century, wealthy New Englanders bought abandoned farms in New Hampshire and turned them into country estates. One such gentleman was John Hay, a friend of Abraham Lincoln. Hay served as U.S. secretary of state from 1898 to 1905. He acquired land on the southern tip of Lake Sunapee near the towns of New London and Newbury. He planted roses, built a rock garden, and called the estate the Fells after a region in Scotland he loved.

When John Hay died in 1906, his son and daughter-in-law took over the property. The couple added delightful fountains and walled terraces. Especially stunning was their garden, where they cultivated exotic plants such as Chinese dogwoods and Japanese torch azaleas. Towering over the garden were sugar maples more than 200 years old. It is no wonder their son John Milton Hay, who grew up on the grounds, became a nature writer. The Hay family donated much of the Fells to New Hampshire in the 1960s, and it is now open to the public. While touring Fells, guests recall a line written by John Milton Hay in his book *The Immortal Wilderness*: "It is an unfortunate man or woman who has never loved a tree." ■

More than 300 species of birds have been recorded in New Hampshire. Frequently seen birds are robins, barn owls, crows, finches, sparrows, warblers, and woodpeckers. Flocks of ducks and geese often cross the sky in majestic formations. Game birds such as ruffed grouse, pheasants, woodcocks, and wild turkeys also live in the state. The bald eagle, a rare bird, is still seen soaring over New Hampshire forests and mountains.

Moose Watching

Moose are huge animals, averaging 1,000 pounds (454 kilograms) and standing 6 feet (2 m) tall at the shoulders. Being the biggest animals in the forest, they have little to fear from predators. Unlike deer, they do not bound away when startled. But do not get too close to these animals. If they sense danger, they may charge you (they run at 40 miles [64 km] an hour), and they use their sharp hooves to stomp a foe. Watch them from the safety of a parked car. ■

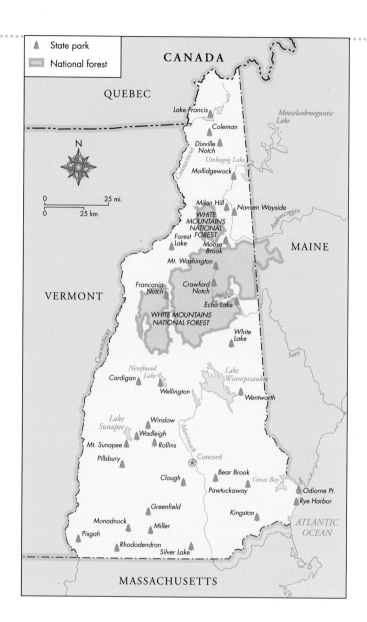

State park
National forest

CANADA

QUEBEC

Lake Francis

Mooselookmeguntic
Lake

Coleman

Dixville
Notch

Umbagog Lake

Mollidgewock

N

0   25 mi.
0   25 km

Milan Hill   Nansen Wayside

Androscoggin

WHITE
MOUNTAINS
NATIONAL
FOREST

MAINE

Forest
Lake   Moose
Brook

Mt. Washington

Franconia
Notch   Crawford
Notch

Saco

VERMONT

Echo Lake

WHITE MOUNTAINS
NATIONAL FOREST

White
Lake

Saco

Newfound
Lake   Lake
Winnipesaukee

Cardigan

Wellington   Wentworth

Lake
Sunapee   Winslow

Wadleigh

Mt. Sunapee   Rollins

Pillsbury   Concord

Clough   Bear Brook

Pawtuckaway   Great Bay

Odiorne Pt.
Rye Harbor

Greenfield

Monadnock   Miller   Kingston   ATLANTIC
OCEAN

Pisgah

Rhododendron   Merrimack

Silver Lake

Connecticut

MASSACHUSETTS

Bats!

Near the town of Gorham in northern New Hampshire is Mascot Mine—a silver mine dug in the 1880s and abandoned many years ago. Today, the mine is home to bats— 1,500 of them at latest count. They hang in the dark cavelike mineshaft during the day and swoop out at night to feed on insects. Some people consider bats to be ugly creatures, but they keep the mosquito population under control. In one nightly feeding, a single bat consumes 3,000 flying bugs. ■

Looking for a good place to fish? Brown, rainbow, and brook trout swim in the state's lakes and streams. Also found are bass, pickerel, and yellow and white perch. Lobsters, oysters, and shrimp live along the coast. Tourist boats take people on whale-watching trips off New Hampshire's shores. Many years ago, the

The Lake Umbagog National Wildlife Refuge

Nature lovers argue about where is the best place to see wildlife in New Hampshire. Many agree that Lake Umbagog National Wildlife Refuge near the town of Errol tops the list. It is both a wetlands and a spruce forest. *Umbagog* is a Native American word meaning "clear waters," and the waters in this reserve are still clear. Moose can be seen drinking from the streams. Leonard Pond within the reserve is the home of the only nesting family of bald eagles known in the state. Other birds inhabiting this wildlife wonderland include loons, kingfishers, and blue herons. ■

Fishing on the Contoocook River

wild Atlantic salmon was common in the state. This salmon lived in the ocean but swam up freshwater streams to spawn. Pollution and the construction of river dams almost eradicated the species, but the wild Atlantic salmon has now been reintroduced in New Hampshire waters and it is hoped the fish will thrive again.

New Hampshire's natural wonders are perhaps its biggest attraction, bringing millions of tourists into the state each year. Once people see the striking forests and mountains of the Granite State, they come back again and again. These return visits give credence to a poem that appeared in a New Hampshire guidebook written in the 1930s:

Every road that leads you out
Makes you long to turn about,
In New Hampshire.

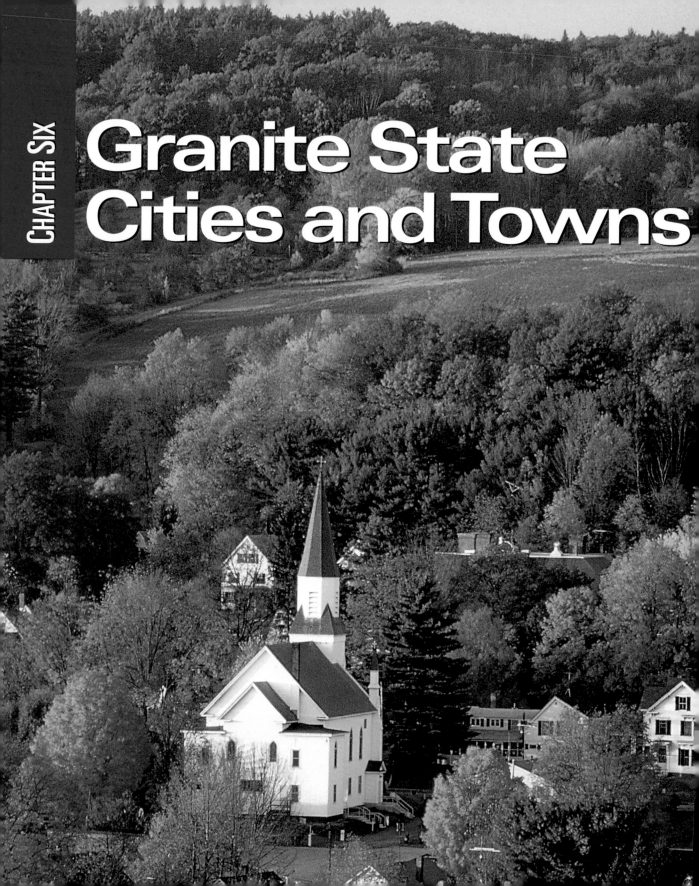

CHAPTER SIX

Granite State Cities and Towns

D on't look for big cities in New Hampshire. The largest city is Manchester, and it doesn't even rank in the top fifty cities of the United States. Instead, New Hampshire is a collection of small to midsize towns. These towns are full of friendly people, and many enjoy an unhurried lifestyle that is sadly lacking in most of the modern world.

Philips Exeter Academy in Exeter

Towns Near the Seacoast

New Hampshire's small (18-mile [29-km]-long) seacoast is the state's historic heart. Most of the towns along the coast and immediately inland were settled hundreds of years ago by English colonists. Today the coastal region towns reflect the pride of those pioneers.

Opposite: The town of Wilton

The oldest of the old towns is Rye. Here, the followers of David Thomson built a settlement just three years after the Pilgrims landed at Plymouth, Massachusetts. The lives of those early settlers were always hard and often dangerous. In 1694, a Rye man named John Locke staged a one-man war against the local Native Americans. Locke boldly drilled holes in the side of a canoe that had been beached by an Indian war party. The Indians discovered their damaged boat and shot and killed Locke with his own gun. Thus ended the one-man war. Today, Rye is a peaceful village and serves as the entrance to Rye Harbor State Park and to Odiorne Point State Park.

Not so peaceful—at least not on the Fourth of July—is the town of Hampton Beach. Every Independence Day, an estimated 150,000 people crowd into this seaside community to enjoy the sun and music and walk the 3-mile (5-km) boardwalk. Aside from the Independence Day bash, Hampton Beach is hailed as one of the prettiest and most serene seashores in all New England. Nearby Hampton, settled in 1638, is another one of the coastal region's "grandfather" towns. The town of Exeter is also steeped in history. When visiting Exeter don't miss the American Independence Museum where the story of the American Revolution unfolds.

Portsmouth is proud of its history, but the city lives solidly in the modern world. Kids enjoy hands-on exhibits at the Children's Museum of Portsmouth. One display at the museum demonstrates the age-old art of catching lobsters. The Portsmouth Harbor Trail leads past many homes built before the United States gained its independence. Portraits and centuries-old furniture are featured at the Moffat-Ladd House, built in 1763.

**Prescott Park
in Portsmouth**

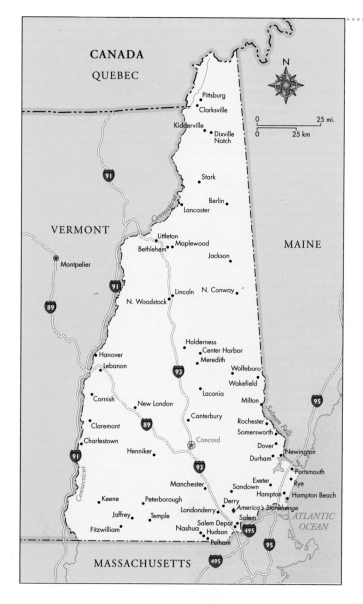

New Hampshire's cities and interstates

Newington was once the home of the huge Pease Air Force Base. Pease closed in the early 1990s, forcing the town to readjust its economy. Newington returned to the attractive coastal region village it had been before the air force moved to town. Durham is home to the University of New Hampshire, where some 14,000 students are busy with their studies. The University of New Hampshire's art gallery has 1,100 paintings and sculptures on permanent display as well as frequent traveling exhibits.

Southern New Hampshire

The south, the most populous region of New Hampshire, is also the fastest-growing. Many people living in the south are recent transplants from Massachusetts. The sudden transformation of southern New Hampshire from a rural region to a place of small cities is called the Massachusetts Miracle.

Derry and Londonderry are two historic towns that have grown in recent years because of their closeness to Massachusetts. If the traffic is right, both towns are about an hour's drive from Boston.

Canobie Lake Park

Near Salem is one of New England's oldest and most popular amusement parks. About a century ago, the Canobie Lake Park offered families scenic rides on streetcars. Today, visitors enjoy thrill-a-minute roller-coaster adventures such as the Yankee Cannonball and the wet and wild Timber Splash Water Coaster. In all, the park has seventy-five rides offering various degrees of fright. Try the Cannonball—if you dare. ■

Derry's population has more than doubled since 1980. Nearby towns such as Salem, Windham, Pelham, and Hudson have also seen rapid growth because of recent arrivals from Massachusetts. The town of Sandown boasts the Sandown Depot Railroad Museum, a favorite among railroad buffs.

In recent years, Nashua has gone from a mill town to a mall town. It serves as the "Gate City" for citizens of Massachusetts eager to shop in New Hampshire where sales taxes do not exist. The Nashua Mall became the state's first enclosed shopping mall when it opened in 1969, but it has since been dwarfed by suburban malls and by shops on Main Street, the city's main thoroughfare. Clothing is the big draw in Nashua. New and excellent restaurants now serve the bargain hunters who flock to this once rather shabby mill town.

Main Street in Nashua

The Currier Gallery of Art is located in Manchester.

Manchester, too, is a city gripped by change. Long gone are the Amoskeag Mills, once the largest employer in the state, but industry still prevails here. In modern Manchester, factories produce computer chips and integrated circuits instead of miles and miles of cloth. The city has fifty parks of various sizes. The Currier Gallery of Art exhibits paintings, furniture, and silver pieces from all over the world. Many experts hail the Currier Gallery as the finest small museum in the United States. The Manchester Historic Association shows artifacts from Indian times to the industrial era.

The tiny town of Peterborough is home to the famous Mac-Dowell Colony. Spreading over 400 acres (162 ha), it is a retreat for artists, writers, and composers. Marian MacDowell, wife of celebrated composer Edward MacDowell, established the colony in the early 1900s. The creative artists work in cabins and get together

The Lawrence E. Lee Scouting Museum

The history of scouting is presented at this Manchester museum. Displays include insignia worn by Cub Scouts, Boy Scouts, and Explorer Scouts. Original paintings that graced the covers of the famous scout magazine *Boys' Life* hang on the walls. The adjoining Max I. Silber Library has a collection of scout yearbooks and magazines dating back to the early 1900s. ■

Downtown Peterborough

in a main building to eat and chat. The composer Leonard Bernstein wrote music while living in the MacDowell Colony. The playwright Thorton Wilder was also a MacDowell Colony guest. In 1938, Wilder wrote his famous play *Our Town* and used Peterborough as the basis for the play's imaginary town of Grover's Corners.

The village of Temple has an outstanding band, which is said to be the oldest town band in the United States. Dublin's early settlers were of Scotch-Irish heritage. Willa Cather (1873–1947), who wrote beloved novels of American pioneer life, often stayed in Jaffrey. She is buried in the town cemetery. Fitzwilliam is such a picturesque New England town that its main street has been used on Christmas cards. Collectors flock to its many antique shops. Charlestown is proud of its cluster of sixty-three historic homes, ten of which were built before 1800. The city of Keene claims that it displays more jack-o'-lanterns on Halloween than any other town in the country. In the 1990s, Keene was rated by several magazines as one of the country's best small towns in which to raise a family.

Central New Hampshire and the Lakes Region

Concord, the state capital, lies in the center of the southern half of the state. It was planned that way in 1808 when leaders wanted a new capital city that would be an easier journey for most of the state's residents than the one to Portsmouth. The highlight of Concord is the capitol. Built in 1819, it is the nation's oldest state capitol in continual use by a legislative body. The building's grounds contain statues of many famous New Hampshire residents including Daniel Webster, Revolutionary War general John Stark, and President Franklin Pierce. Nearby is the fascinating Museum of New Hampshire History and a famous library—the New Hampshire Historical Society.

North of Concord is Canterbury, home of the Shaker Village. The Shakers were a religious sect that began in the 1700s. Their prayer sessions were so intense they caused participants to quiver and shake, hence the sect's name. In the 1780s, the Shakers established a village at Canterbury. At its peak in 1860, approximately 300 people lived there on grounds that spread over 4,000 acres (1,620 ha). In 1992, the last survivor of the Shaker Village, Sister Ethel Hudson, died at age ninety-six. Today, the Shaker Village at Canterbury is a living museum. Guests are invited to see how the Shakers lived according to their creed, "Hands to Work and Hearts to God."

The Shaker Village in Canterbury is now a museum.

Hanover is home to 6,000 students studying at Dartmouth College. Dartmouth was chartered in 1769 to educate Native Americans and ranks as the ninth-oldest college in the United States. The college enriches Hanover's culture with its symphony orchestra, its theater group, and the Hood Museum of Art. South of Hanover is Cornish, famed for its four covered bridges.

The Henniker Ghost

Families arriving in the 1750s settled the town of Henniker. One of Henniker's most famous residents, Mary Wallace, rests in the town cemetery. Mary Wallace was born at sea in 1710, on a ship sailing toward New Hampshire. Shortly after her birth, a pirate crew captured the vessel. Seeing the lovely baby in her mother's arms melted the pirate captain's heart. The captain promised not to harm the ship if the mother would name the baby Mary, after his dead wife. The captain even gave the mother a bundle of silk to be used for Mary's wedding dress. Mary Wallace married while wearing a dress made from the silk, settled in Henniker, and lived to be an old lady. A story says her ghostly figure can still be seen on moonlit nights, waiting to thank the pirate for his mercy. ■

Claremont, once a gritty mill town, is today enjoying a rebirth as a tourist center for the lovely region along the Sugar River. Take a look at Claremont's 100-year-old opera house, which has been recently restored to its former grandeur. Water everywhere describes the town of New London. The town rests on an arm of Lake Sunapee, and residents can stroll the shores of two smaller lakes within the New London borders. Rochester is a proud old town whose roots date back to 1728 when a settler named Captain Timothy Roberts began to farm here.

Claremont is enjoying renewed life as a tourist center.

Inside Claremont's
famous opera house

A highlight of New Hampshire's Lakes Region is the sprawling Lake Winnipesaukee, named by the Abenaki Indians. It is a popular destination for summer vacationers.

Laconia, at the southern end of the Lakes Region, is an old industrial village that now serves tourists. More than 100,000 motorcyclists descend on Laconia each year for Motorcycle Week—the annual motorcycle races held at the nearby New Hampshire Speedway racetrack. Tourists also flock to Wolfeboro, where city leaders claim the town's population rises tenfold each June when the summer visitors arrive. Less crowded, at least in the past, was the town of Holderness. Then in 1981, the popular movie *On Golden Pond* was shot nearby. Now crowds of movie fans come to Holderness and to neighboring villages such as Center Harbor and Meredith.

Two Museums

Two interesting museums entertain visitors to the Lakes Region. The New Hampshire Farm Museum (above), near Milton, displays 60,000 items from farm life of the late 1700s to 1900. The Museum of Childhood, at Wakefield, delights kids with its antique model trains, hundreds of dolls, and forty-four furnished dollhouses. Adults come to relive their childhood. ◼

The White Mountains and the North

Everyone thinks of the White Mountains as wild country, and the region is one of the wildest sections of land you'll find in the eastern United States. But the White Mountains National Forest embraces forty-nine towns. Many of these mountain villages surprise visitors with their charm.

The town of Jackson serves White Mountain tourists year-round. In the summer, tourists come to this storybook New England village to browse in the antique shops; in the winter, Jackson is a focal point for cross-country skiers. Fantastic mountain views draw visitors to the historic town of Bartlett, incorporated in 1790. The towns of North Woodstock and Lincoln are gateways for people rugged enough to trek over the 1,200 miles (1,930 km) of hiking trails that cross the White Mountains.

Bethlehem is a White Mountain town, founded in the 1780s and named after the holy city in the New Testament. In 1863, a wealthy Rhode Island man rode through here on a stagecoach. The stagecoach tipped over on the rugged mountain trail, and the Rhode Island gentleman was forced to spend several weeks in Bethlehem recovering from his injuries. He was so overwhelmed by the region's beauty that he built several summer hotels here, and Bethlehem has been a tourist center ever since. Nearby is Maplewood, another White Mountain village with a story to tell. From about 1900 to 1950, impoverished boys from an industrial school in Boston came to a golf course in Maplewood to take summer jobs as caddies and groundskeepers. Some of those inner-city boys had police records, but they became successful in later life. To this day, the one-time golf-course employees hold reunions in Maplewood.

Berlin, with a population of about 12,000, is the largest town in northern New Hampshire. Unlike other towns whose economy has gone from mills to malls, Berlin remains an industrial center. For the past 150 years, Berlin has been a logging town with paper mills as its major business. Berlin is sometimes called "the City That Trees Built." A visitor will find many interesting towns near Berlin. Errol (named after a region in Scotland) sits on the Androscoggin River and is a magnet for canoeists and rafters. Stark is known for its covered bridge and church, both built in the 1850s, and is one of the most photographed small towns in the state. Lancaster, near the Connecticut River, is a popular shopping center.

Stark's church and covered bridge have been photographed over and over again.

In the far north are the towns of Dixville Notch, Colebrook, Clarksville, and Pittsburg. Few tourists venture this far north in New Hampshire, and the roads are refreshingly uncrowded. A portion of Route 3, which runs to Pittsburg, is called Moose Alley because of frequent moose sightings along the highway. The town of Dixville Notch lies at the entrance to the lovely Dixville Notch State Park.

CHAPTER SEVEN

Governing the Granite State

The Hall of Flags in the capitol

Unique! Independent! Different! All these one-word descriptions apply to New Hampshire's state government. The Granite State government is a shining example of how New Hampshirites insist upon doing things their own special way.

The Different State

Like that of other states, New Hampshire's government is divided into three branches: the executive, the legislative, and the judicial. The governor heads the executive branch. It is the governor's job to carry out, or enforce, laws. The legislative department is made up of elected lawmakers who are divided into two bodies, or houses: the New Hampshire house of representatives and the senate. The legislature creates new laws and rescinds old laws. The judicial department consists of the court system. The courts hear cases and make sure new laws are true to the state constitution.

Opposite: The capitol in Concord

The government of New Hampshire is structured like that of other states, and its framework is similar to that of the national government. But the details of the Granite State government are a little different.

First, the New Hampshire legislature is called the General Court, which makes it sound as if it is part of the judicial system. It inherited that confusing name from Massachusetts more than 200 years ago. The General Court's senate has 24 members, while the house of representatives has a whopping 400 members, making it the largest such body in the fifty states. Yet such a huge house of representatives does not cost the government a great deal. Legislators are paid only $100 a year, the same as they were paid before the Civil War. No one can make a living on $100 a year of course. Most lawmakers are professional people who own businesses or hold other jobs.

Both houses of the General Court can propose laws, called bills. If a majority of both houses approve, the bill goes to the governor for his or her signature. Once the governor signs it, the bill

Meet the Governor

Governor Jeanne Shaheen (1947–) is typical of the "new" New Hampshirites, in that she came here from somewhere else. Shaheen was born in Missouri, went to college in Pennsylvania, and moved to New Hampshire in 1973. After serving three terms in the state senate, she was elected governor in 1996 and reelected in 1998. In addition to her political career, Shaheen has worked as a schoolteacher, and she ran a small silver and leather business with her husband. Shaheen was the first woman governor elected in New Hampshire. ■

becomes a law. The governor may veto, or decline to sign, a bill. In the event of a veto, the bill is returned to the legislative department. If both the senate and the house of representatives re-approve the bill by a two-thirds vote, the bill becomes a law regardless of the governor's veto.

The New Hampshire supreme court is the guardian of the state constitution. If the supreme court determines that a law violates the constitution, the judges have the right to declare the law null and void. In October 1999, the state supreme court claimed a property tax law was unconstitutional because, in the court's opinion, the law gave wealthier communities what amounted to a tax break. The law

The New Hampshire supreme court in session

New Hampshire's Governors

Name	Party	Term	Name	Party	Term
Meshech Weare	None	1776–1785	William Haile	Rep.	1857–1859
John Langdon	None	1785–1786	Ichabod Goodwin	Rep.	1859–1861
John Sullivan	Fed.	1786–1788	Nathaniel S. Berry	Rep.	1861–1863
John Langdon	Dem.-Rep.	1788–1789	Joseph A. Gilmore	Rep.	1863–1865
John Sullivan	Fed.	1789–1790	Frederick Smyth	Rep.	1865–1867
Josiah Bartlett	Dem.-Rep.	1790–1794	Walter Harriman	Rep.	1867–1869
John T. Gilman	Fed.	1794–1805	Onslow Stearns	Rep.	1869–1871
John Langdon	Dem.-Rep.	1805–1809	James A. Weston	Dem.	1871–1872
Jeremiah Smith	Fed.	1809–1810	Ezekiel A. Straw	Rep.	1872–1874
John Langdon	Dem.-Rep.	1810–1812	James A. Weston	Dem.	1874–1875
William Plumer	Dem.-Rep.	1812–1813	Person C. Cheney	Rep.	1875–1877
John T. Gilman	Fed.	1813–1816	Benjamin F. Prescott	Rep.	1877–1879
William Plumer	Dem.-Rep.	1816–1819	Natt Head	Rep.	1879–1881
Samuel Bell	Dem.-Rep.	1819–1823	Charles H. Bell	Rep.	1881–1883
Levi Woodbury	Dem.-Rep.	1823–1824	Samuel W. Hale	Rep.	1883–1885
David L. Morrill	Dem.-Rep.	1824–1827	Moody Currier	Rep.	1885–1887
Benjamin Pierce	Dem.-Rep.	1827–1828	Charles H. Sawyer	Rep.	1887–1889
John Bell	Nat. Rep.	1828–1829	David H. Goodell	Rep.	1889–1891
Benjamin Pierce	Dem.	1829–1830	Hiram A. Tuttle	Rep.	1891–1893
Matthew Harvey	Dem.	1830–1831	John B. Smith	Rep.	1893–1895
Samuel Dinsmoor	Dem.	1831–1834	Charles A. Busiel	Rep.	1895–1897
William Badger	Dem.	1834–1836	George A. Ramsdell	Rep.	1897–1899
Isaac Hill	Dem.	1836–1839	Frank W. Rollins	Rep.	1899–1901
John Page	Dem.	1839–1842	Chester B. Jordan	Rep.	1901–1903
Henry Hubbard	Dem.	1842–1844	Nahum J. Batchelder	Rep.	1903–1905
John H. Steele	Dem.	1844–1846	John McLane	Rep.	1905–1907
Anthony Colby	Whig	1846–1847	Charles M. Floyd	Rep.	1907–1909
Jared W. Williams	Dem.	1847–1849	Henry B. Quinby	Rep.	1909–1911
Samuel Dinsmoor Jr.	Dem.	1849–1852	Robert P. Bass	Rep.	1911–1913
Noah Martin	Dem.	1852–1854	Samuel D. Felker	Dem.	1913–1915
Nathaniel B. Baker	Dem.	1854–1855	Rolland H. Spaulding	Rep.	1915–1917
Ralph Metcalf	Am.	1855–1857	Henry W. Keyes	Rep.	1917–1919

New Hampshire's Governors (continued)

Name	Party	Term	Name	Party	Term
John H. Bartlett	Rep.	1919–1921	Hugh Gregg	Rep.	1953–1955
Albert O. Brown	Rep.	1921–1923	Lane Dwinell	Rep.	1955–1959
Fred H. Brown	Dem.	1923–1925	Wesley Powell	Rep.	1959–1963
John G. Winant	Rep.	1925–1927	John W. King	Dem.	1963–1969
Huntley N. Spaulding	Rep.	1927–1929	Walter R. Peterson Jr.	Rep.	1969–1973
Charles W. Tobey	Rep.	1929–1931	Meldrim Thomson Jr.	Rep.	1973–1979
John G. Winant	Rep.	1931–1935	Hugh J. Gallen	Dem.	1979–1982
Styles Bridges	Rep.	1935–1937	John H. Sununu	Rep.	1983–1989
Francis P. Murphy	Rep.	1937–1941	Judd Gregg	Rep.	1989–1993
Robert O. Blood	Rep.	1941–1945	Steve Merrill	Rep.	1993–1997
Charles M. Dale	Rep.	1945–1949	Jeanne Shaheen	Dem.	1997–
Sherman Adams	Rep.	1949–1953			

involved $825 million promised for education. The court's action shocked residents because taxes of any sort are a very sensitive subject in New Hampshire.

The structure of government is determined by the state constitution, which took effect in 1784. That constitution is three years older than the U.S. Constitution. Items in the constitution have been amended, or changed, many times over the years. Amendments require a two-thirds vote of the people.

All citizens eighteen years or older who have resided in the state for more than ten days are entitled to vote. The governor runs for reelection every two years. The governor is assisted by a five-member executive council whose members are elected to two-year terms. The attorney general, who is appointed by the governor with approval of the executive council, is another important mem-

New Hampshire's State Government

Executive Branch

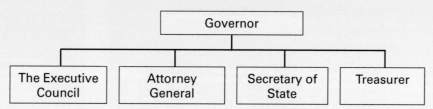

Unlike most other states, New Hampshire does not have a lieutenant governor; the president of the senate serves as governor in case of the governor's death or discharge from office.

Legislative Branch

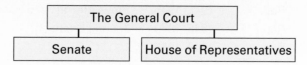

Judicial Branch

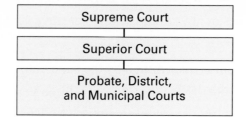

ber of the executive branch. Representatives in the General Court serve two-year terms. The governor appoints members to the supreme court for life.

New Hampshire has ten counties. All towns are ruled by town meetings held once a year. Elected leaders in towns are called selectmen, even though they are often women. Towns and cities have the important functions of maintaining roads, providing police, and delivering other services to citizens.

Dixville Notch is a tiny community of about 100 people in northern New Hampshire. Every four years in February, television crews descend on this sleepy town in the middle of the night and set up cameras. Often the town is buried in snow. Why does the media come here? The polling places in Dixville Notch open at midnight on primary day, making these voters the very first U.S. citizens to cast ballots for a presidential hopeful. ■

Politics and Primaries

In 1999, Vice President Al Gore and former U.S. senator Bill Bradley debated in Hanover. Each man wanted to become president. The debate took place in October when the presidential

Bill Bradley (left) and Vice President Al Gore shaking hands in Hanover

elections were more than a year away. Why such intensive campaigning so far from election day? This is New Hampshire, where primary elections come early.

The purpose of a primary election is to narrow the field of candidates. For example, seven or eight people may run for office in a primary election, but only the two top vote-getters will be major candidates in the general election. Most states hold primary elections shortly before the general election. New Hampshire primaries come in February, a full nine months ahead of election day. Since 1920, the New Hampshire primaries have been the nation's first. Politicians who hope to become president

Jimmy Carter (standing) campaigned in New Hampshire before being elected president in 1976.

must begin their journey to the White House in the Granite State.

The early primaries in New Hampshire have proved to be a remarkable barometer for later elections. For forty years, from 1952 to 1992, no candidate won the presidency without first winning the New Hampshire primaries. New Hampshirites enjoy the attention they receive because of their early primaries. It is said that, if you hang around Main Street in Concord or Elm Street in Manchester long enough, you are bound to meet someone who— someday—will be president of the United States. The zeal to be the nation's first voters led one writer to suggest the Granite State ought to change its motto from "Live Free or Die" to "Vote First or Die."

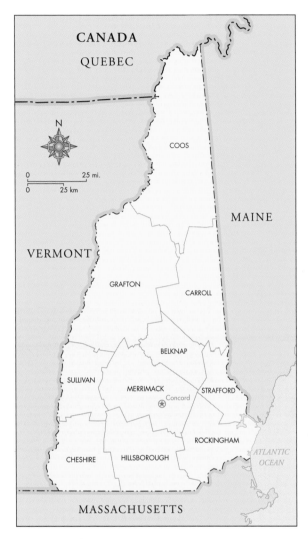

New Hampshire's counties

The political preferences of New Hampshirites are changing with the influx of new people. Traditionally, Yankees were conservative and tended to vote Republican. Through most of the twentieth century, Granite State voters elected Republican governors and voted for Republican presidents. This pattern began to change in the 1990s. Democratic presidential candidate Bill Clinton carried the state in 1992, even though he had lost the New Hampshire primary that year. Jeanne Shaheen, a Democrat, was elected governor in 1996. Today, New Hampshire has a balance between Democratic and Republican voters.

New Hampshire's State Symbols

State bird: Purple finch Finches belong to five families. About one in seven of the birds flying about the planet are finches. The purple finch (above), which is abundant in the eastern United States, is known for its sweet song.

State animal: White-tailed deer Deer live in all parts of New Hampshire. The white-tailed deer, a very common animal in the state, is so named because it flashes its white tail when running.

State insect: Ladybug "Ladybug, ladybug fly away home; your house is on fire . . ." These colorful, harmless insects inspire poetry and song. The legislature adopted the ladybug as the state insect in 1977 at the urging of the fifth-grade class of the Broken Grounds Grammar School in Concord.

State tree: White birch This tree is sometimes called the paper birch because its bark is thin and easy to write upon when peeled off. New Hampshire Indians used white birch for the outsides of their birch-bark canoes. A mature white birch grows 50 to 70 feet (15 to 21 m) tall.

New Hampshire's State Flag and Seal

New Hampshire's state flag shows the state seal against a blue field. Surrounding the state seal is a laurel wreath and nine stars, which indicate that New Hampshire was the ninth state to ratify the U.S. Constitution. In the center of the seal is a picture of the U.S. warship *Raleigh*, which fought in the Revolutionary War. The *Raleigh* was built in Portsmouth. This state flag was approved in 1909. ■

State amphibian: Red-spotted newt A newt (right) is a type of salamander. It lives freely on both land and water. The red-spotted newt is a small creature with a thin body and four legs. As the name implies, the red-spotted newt has a reddish color.

State gem: Smoky quartz Quartz is a material found in rocks that looks like broken glass. Smoky quartz has a dazzling sparkle and is either black or brown.

State rock: Granite Highly prized for its toughness, granite is used in building bridges, thick-walled structures such as banks, and monuments. Granite is the bedrock of all New Hampshire.

State flower: Purple lilac The lilac is a shrub that blossoms in the spring with beautiful, sweet-smelling flowers. The Wentworth-Coolidge Mansion, a charming old house in Portsmouth, is famous for its lilacs, which were brought from England more than two centuries ago. Some say they were the first lilacs transplanted from the Old World.

State freshwater fish: Brook trout Adopted as a state symbol in 1992, the brook trout is plentiful in New Hampshire's rivers and lakes.

State saltwater fish: Striped bass Adopted as a state symbol in 1992, the striped bass swim in New Hampshire's coastal waters.

New Hampshire's State Song
"Old New Hampshire"

"Old New Hampshire" was written in 1926 (words by Dr. John Holmes and music by Maurie Hoffman) and adopted as the official state song in 1949. New Hampshire also has eight honorary songs, which rank slightly below the official state song. The eight honorary songs are: "New Hampshire, My New Hampshire," "New Hampshire Hills," "Autumn in New Hampshire," "New Hampshire's Granite State," "Oh, New Hampshire (You're My Home)," "The Old Man of the Mountain," "The New Hampshire State March," and "New Hampshire Naturally."

*With a skill that knows no
   measure
From the golden store of fate
God, in His great love and wis-
   dom,
Made the rugged Granite State;
Made the lakes, the fields, the
   forests;
Made the rivers and the rills;
Made the bubbling, crystal
   fountains
Of New Hampshire's Granite
   Hills.*

*Refrain
Old New Hampshire, Old New
   Hampshire
Old New Hampshire grand
   and great
We will sing of Old New
   Hampshire
Of the dear old Granite State
Builded He New Hampshire
   glorious
From the borders to the sea
And with matchless charm
   and splendor*

*Blessed He for eternity.
Hers, the majesty of mountains;
Hers, the grandeur of the
   lake;
Hers, the truth as from the
   hillside
Whence her crystal waters
   break.*

Refrain

State Emblem

New Hampshire's famous profile, the stony face of the Old Man of the Mountain, is at the center of the state emblem. Above the face are the words STATE OF NEW HAMPSHIRE, below it is the state motto: LIVE FREE OR DIE.

Woodchuck Bounty

In 1883, New Hampshire officials believed woodchucks were harming crops, so the government offered a bounty on the animals. Hunters were paid a certain sum of money every time they brought a dead woodchuck to authorities. In less than two years, the state discontinued the program because the woodchuck bounty had exhausted the treasury. ■

Taxes and Finances

In the late 1990s, a typical one-year state budget for New Hampshire was approximately $2.5 billion. The education budget alone was $825 million. Where does this money come from? New Hampshire gets some money from the federal government, but never enough. In most states, the cost of government is raised largely through state income taxes, which deducts taxes from workers' paychecks, and a state sales tax, which shoppers pay when buying an item at a store. But in New Hampshire the words "income tax" and "sales tax" border on foul language.

New Hampshire and Alaska are the only two states in the United States that have no income tax and no sales tax. Alaska has less of a need for such taxes because of that state's huge oil reserves; the Alaskan government collects a percentage of every barrel of oil that is pumped from the ground. New Hampshire has no such resource.

State leaders in the Granite State have to be creative to raise money. In 1964, New Hampshire became the first state to hold a lottery to finance the school budget. Today, more than 1,200 stores

Many New Hampshire stores sell lottery tickets.

sell state lottery tickets. The state also gets money from visitors through special taxes on hotel rooms. Taxes on gasoline are higher than in most other states and especially high taxes are placed on alcohol and tobacco sales. As one state official said, "We tax sin."

Low taxes are one of the lures that bring new people and businesses to the Granite State. Many ex-Massachusetts residents scornfully call their old state "Taxachusetts." But many believe that someday New Hampshire will have to ask its citizens to pay income taxes or sales taxes, or both. In the meantime, candidates for governor and other high offices routinely take "the pledge"—an unofficial promise not to impose taxes on citizens of the Granite State.

Political Families

to 1993 and was elected U.S. senator from New Hampshire in 1992. John H. Sununu (below) was governor from 1983 to 1989 and later served as White House chief of staff for President George Bush; his son, John E. Sununu Jr., was elected to the U.S. House of Representatives in 1996. ■

Two of the most powerful political families in New Hampshire are the Greggs and the Sununus. Both are Republican, and both have had fathers and sons in high elective offices. Hugh Gregg served as governor from 1953 to 1955; his son, Judd Gregg (above), was governor from 1989

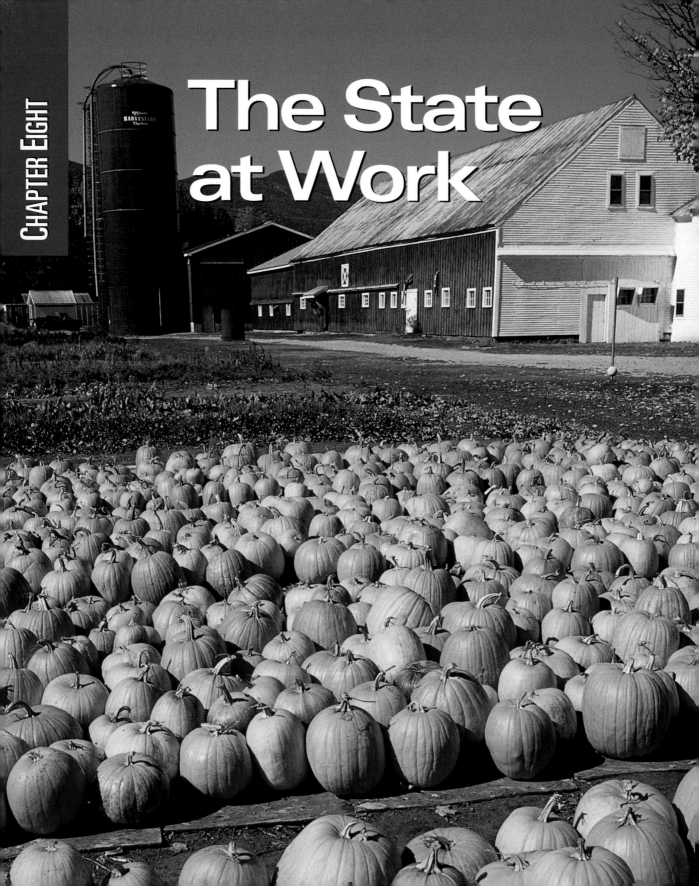

CHAPTER EIGHT

The State at Work

A paper mill in
Groveton

The Granite State was not blessed with rich farmland or abundant natural resources. Creativity was always necessary to make a living here. Over the last 200 years, the economy shifted from agriculture to manufacturing to high-tech industry, and each stage of the transition was successful. Today, New Hampshire has one of highest standards of living of all the fifty states.

Goods from the Factories

Some 117,000 New Hampshire workers—about one-fifth of the workforce—hold manufacturing jobs. In the past, those workers produced cotton cloth and other textiles. Today, they are more likely to assemble electric machinery and space-age products.

Opposite: A pumpkin
farm in North Conway

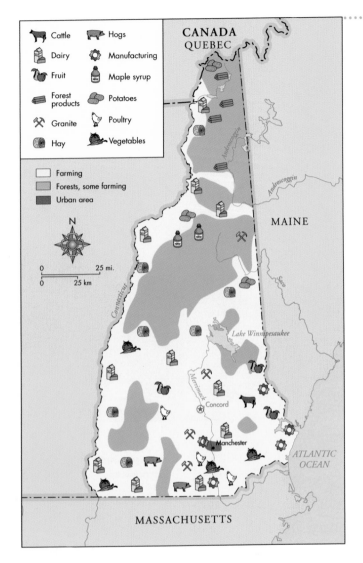

New Hampshire's
natural resources

Factories in Hudson, Manchester, Merrimack, Nashua, Portsmouth, and Salem make computers. Scientific instruments and delicate tools used in hospitals are made in various parts of the state. Traditional "smokestack" industries are not forgotten in the modern economy. Plants in Peterborough and Keene make ball bearings. Foundries operate in Milford. Boots and footwear, an old-time industry in New Hampshire, are made at the Timberland Company's plant in Hampton. Lamps are manufactured in Manchester. Food-processing remains a major business. Soft drinks are made in Bedford, and beer is brewed in Merrimack.

Goods from the Land

New Hampshire has about 2,000 farms, mostly small family farms that cover an average of 179 acres (72 ha). Less than 1 percent of the state's workforce is employed in farming. Hay and vegetables are the chief field crops. Dairy farms are concentrated along the Connecticut River on the state's western border. Beef cattle, eggs, poultry, and hogs are also raised in New Hampshire. Apples are the leading fruit grown in the state. Many farmers sell vegetables, strawberries, raspberries, flowers, and shrubs from roadside stands.

Heidelberg Harris

Heidelberg Harris makes many models of printing presses of various sizes and widths. Some are small machines operated by one printer. Other presses print newspapers and magazines at astonishing speeds. Those presses can be as long as a house. Heidelberg built its Dover plant in 1909 and it now employs 900 people. It is listed as the fifteenth largest employer in New Hampshire. ▪

Only about 400 men and women are employed in mining. Sand, gravel, and crushed stone are major products of the mines. Granite, which gives the state its nickname, remains an important resource. Forest products are also a major industry. Some 85 percent of New Hampshire's forests are owned by lumber companies. Logging and lumber mills employ 16,000 workers.

Cattle are among the livestock raised on New Hampshire farms.

Sawing timber at
a lumber mill

Services and Other Industries

A service worker does not contribute to making a product. Instead a service worker provides a service for a customer. A bagger at a supermarket is a service worker, as is a doctor or a schoolteacher. By far the largest numbers of New Hampshire's workers are service workers—about 183,100. Tourism is largely a service industry because it generates jobs in hotels and restaurants. Each year, tourists spend more than $3 billion in New Hampshire. Some

What New Hampshire Grows, Manufactures, and Mines

Agriculture	Manufacturing	Mining
Apples	Electrical equipment	Granite
Milk	Machinery	Sand and gravel
	Scientific instruments	

New Hampshire Easy Apple Cake

New Hampshire produces some of the finest apples in the United States. This delicious treat should please dessert-lovers to the core.

Ingredients:

- 4 apples, peeled and sliced
- 1/4 cup of sugar; a separate 1/2 cup of sugar
- 1/2 teaspoon cinnamon
- 2 tablespoons soft butter or margarine
- 1 egg
- 1/4 teaspoon vanilla
- 1 cup flour
- 1 teaspoon baking powder

Directions:

Preheat the oven to 350°F. With a little butter or shortening, grease the inside bottom and sides of a baking dish.

Mix together the 1/4 cup of sugar and cinnamon in a bowl.

Place one layer of apples in the baking dish and sprinkle with half the sugar-cinnamon mixture. Lay the remaining apples over this and sprinkle with the other half of the sugar-cinnamon.

In a separate bowl, combine the 1/2 cup of sugar and butter, until creamy. Add the egg and vanilla. Mix well. Stir in flour and baking powder. Spoon evenly over the apples.

Bake for 30 minutes.

The New Hampshire
Turnpike runs along
the state's coastline.

79,700 New Hampshire residents hold government jobs either for the state, the cities, or the federal government.

An efficient transportation system is required to keep the economy functioning. New Hampshire has about 15,000 miles (24,135 km) of roads and highways. Major highways include Interstate 95, which runs along the seacoast, the Everett Turnpike, which links Concord to Massachusetts, and Interstate 89, which connects Concord with Vermont. Trains carry freight to New Hampshire towns, but passenger use has declined. The state once

Maple Syrup, Harvest of the Trees

More than 300 years ago, Native Americans taught New England colonists to boil the sap of maple trees and produce sugary syrup. Today, maple syrup from Vermont and New Hampshire is famous throughout the world. Red maples and sugar maples produce the best syrup. The thick syrup is delicious when poured over pancakes. One small town in the White Mountains, suitably named Sugar Hill, is celebrated for the fine quality of its maple syrup. ■

The Mount Washington Cog Railway

Though train service has diminished, thousands of tourists enjoy taking the cog railway to the top of Mount Washington. A cog railroad is designed to climb steep grades. The Mount Washington Cog Railroad was built in 1869. Today, it is used exclusively to take people on exciting three-hour trips to the peak of the highest mountain in New England. All aboard! ■

had 1,200 miles (1,930 km) of railroad track. Only 470 miles (756 km) of track are in service today. New Hampshire has forty-two airports; the largest is Manchester Airport.

The state's first newspaper, the *New Hampshire Gazette*, was published in Portsmouth in 1756. Modern New Hampshire has fifty-five daily and weekly papers. The *Union Leader* of Manchester is one of the state's most influential papers. Other newspapers include the *Portsmouth Herald*, the *Nashua Telegraph*, and the *Concord Monitor*. Approximately thirty radio stations and ten television stations operate in the state. New Hampshire's first television station was WMUR-TV, which began operations in Manchester in 1954 and is still an active broadcaster.

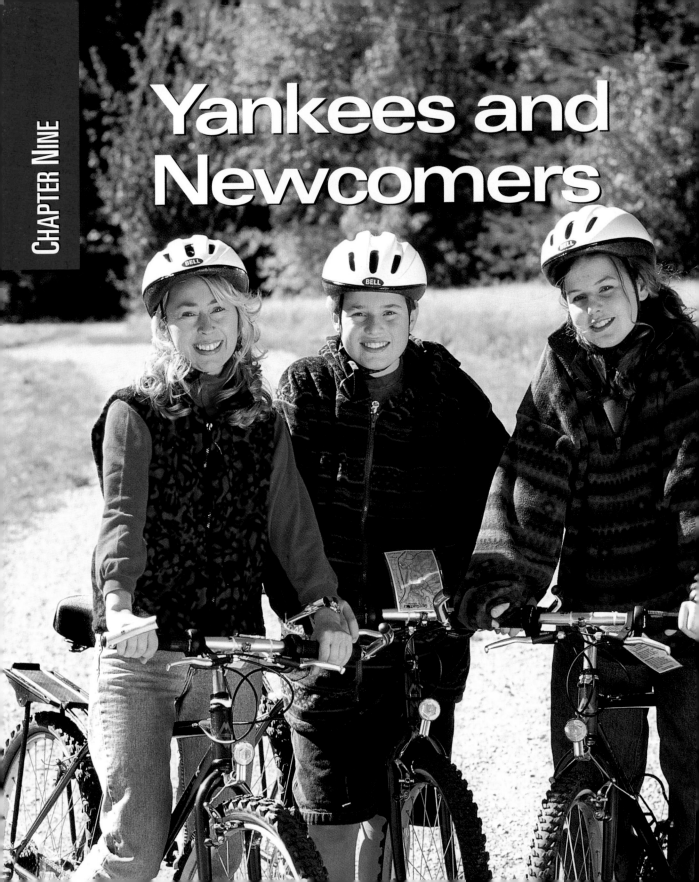

CHAPTER NINE

Yankees and Newcomers

In 1999, Hugh Gregg, the former governor of New Hampshire, attended dinner at a fancy Mexican restaurant in Nashua. Gregg said, "[The place] was mobbed . . . the customers were all high-tech people, young people, full of pep and energy." Gregg is from an old-line Yankee whose family has deep roots in the Granite State. He is also eighty-one years old and can remember when restaurants in Nashua served little more than meat and potatoes. Gregg enjoyed the evening, but he was astounded by the changes that have overwhelmed his state in the last few decades. "Who ever heard of a Mexican restaurant in Nashua?" he exclaimed. Actually, the city has three or four Mexican restaurants and many fine Chinese restaurants too. This diversity is typical of the *new* New Hampshire.

New Hampshire residents at a town meeting

Opposite: Biking on Great Glen Trails

Who Are the New Hampshirites?

In 1950, New Hampshire had a population of 533,242 people. Most were Yankees, descendants of pioneers who settled the state generations ago. Many French-Canadians and ethnic Europeans worked in big-city factories, but the dominant culture of the state was Yankee. Then, in the latter half of the twentieth century, a wave of newcomers brought variety as well as progress.

The state's population has more than doubled since 1950. It jumped 20 percent between 1980 and 1990 alone, making it the nation's sixth fastest growing state on a percentage basis. Most of the increase was a result of people moving to New Hampshire. In 1990, less than half the people were born here; the rest came from outside the state.

Despite the migration of recent years, the population has remained predominantly white. The majority of whites are of British heritage, followed by French or French-Canadians and Germans. According to the 1990 census, 98 percent of New Hampshirites white, about 1 percent Hispanic, and less than 1 percent each African-Americans or Asian and Pacific Islanders.

Martin Luther King Jr. Day

In May 1999, the New Hampshire house of representatives voted to recognize Martin Luther King Jr. Day as a state holiday. New Hampshire was one of the last states in the United States to create such a holiday in recognition of the civil rights leader. The prime sponsor of the Martin Luther King Jr. Bill was Lionel Johnson, one of the few African-American legislators in the General Court. ■

Over the years, New Hampshirites have been church-going people. In pioneer times, churches were called meetinghouses and doubled as places where townspeople could assemble to vote on public matters. Prevalent among the Yankees were Congregationalists, Anglicans, Baptists, and Quakers. Today, nearly one-third of the population is Roman Catholic. Jewish synagogues and Greek Orthodox churches stand in the cities.

Picturesque churches are found throughout the state.

Cathedral of the Pines

Among the most stunning places to worship in this or any other state is the Cathedral of the Pines in the town of Rindge. It is an outdoor church, open to all religions. Surrounded by tall pine trees, it provides an incredible view of Mount Monadnock. The church is dedicated to Sanderson Sloane, whose plane was shot down over Germany in World War II. It is now a national memorial. ■

Population of New Hampshire's Major Cities (1990)

Manchester	99,567
Nashua	79,662
Concord	36,006
Rochester	26,630
Portsmouth	25,925
Dover	25,042

Where Do the People Live?

The 1990 census counted 1,113,915 people living in New Hampshire. This number ranked New Hampshire forty-first in population among the fifty states. The estimated 1998 population was 1,185,000. Experts agree the state will continue to enjoy rapid population growth in the future.

The people of New Hampshire represent a growing variety of ages and backgrounds.

Mary Baker Eddy

The medical establishment was outraged in 1875 when an obscure New Hampshire woman named Mary Baker Eddy (1821–1910) published a book called *Science and Health with Key to the Scriptures*. Eddy, who owned a home in Concord, claimed a sick person could get well by praying to God. What foolishness, said the doctors. Yet Eddy, who often had episodes of poor health, lived to be almost ninety. Mary Baker Eddy was the founder of a new religion called Christian Science and the Church of Christ, Scientist. ■

For most of the twentieth century, the majority of New Hampshirites have lived in cities and towns. According to the 1990 census, 51 percent of residents lived in cities and towns, while 49 percent were rural dwellers. New Hampshire's largest city is Manchester with almost 100,000 people. The smallest town is a cluster of houses called Harts Location with only 28 persons.

Manchester is the state's largest city.

In 1990, the population density of the state as a whole was 120 persons per square mile (46 per sq km). Neighboring Massachusetts had 730 persons per square mile (282 per sq km). Statistics show that New Hampshire is getting crowded though. In 1960, its population density was 67.7 persons per square mile (26 per sq km), or about half what it is now.

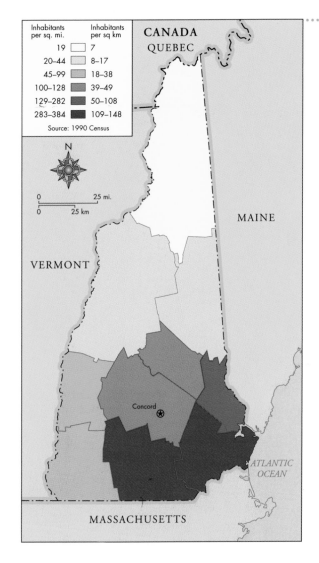

New Hampshire's
population density

New Hampshire residents are concentrated along the seacoast and in the south and the southeast—the area where many newcomers have moved in recent years. The region is so high-tech oriented that a joke says the seacoast ought to be called the "e-coast," for the many electronic and Internet firms that have located there.

Schools and Quality of Life

"Quality of life" is a term that was born in the 1960s when U.S. residents began to have serious concerns about pollution, crime, poverty, and the caliber of their schools. People in certain regions of the country boasted their quality of life was superior to that in other places. In the past, New Hampshirites enjoyed the astonishing beauty offered by their surroundings, but a sluggish economy tore at other quality-of-life issues. Many residents, especially in rural New Hampshire, lived in poverty. Today the state's natural beauty remains, and a vastly improved economy has eased the sufferings of the poor.

New Hampshire has done a remarkable job of reducing poverty. In 1997, only 7.7 percent of the New Hampshire population lived below the poverty level. This figure ranked New Hampshire number one among the states in terms of having the fewest people living in poverty. In 1997, the average yearly income of a

New Hampshire resident was $28,202, the ninth-highest figure among the states.

Poverty breeds crime. In 1996, New Hampshire ranked third in the nation in fewest crimes reported. Cities are often centers of criminal activity. A 1999 study published by *Money* magazine listed Nashua as having the nation's second-lowest rate of violent crimes and Portsmouth as having the fourth lowest. A 1998 crime statistics report from the Morgan Quinto Corporation listed New Hampshire as being one of the safest states in which to live.

A school field trip to Odiorne Point State Park

The University of New Hampshire is located in Durham.

An efficient and caring school system lies at the heart of quality-of-life concerns for most families, and New Hampshire's school system is one of the best in the United States. Year after year, New Hampshire students finish high in tests of reading, math, and science. About 85 percent of New Hampshire's adult residents are high school graduates, and 27 percent have graduated from college.

By law, children in New Hampshire must attend school from age six through sixteen. The state has more than 700 public primary and secondary schools as well as 132 private schools. In 1998, the state had 200,037 students attending public primary and secondary schools. The average classroom size was 15.6 students per teacher.

The state has thirty schools of higher education. The oldest of these is Dartmouth

College, whose charter was signed by England's King George III in 1769. In order of enrollment, the largest schools of higher learning are: University of New Hampshire (Durham), Dartmouth College (Hanover), Keene State College (Keene), New Hampshire College (Manchester), Plymouth State College (Plymouth), River College (Nashua), and St. Anselm College (Manchester).

Decent schools, low crime, and prosperity are all quality-of-life issues. It is no wonder that thousands of new people, especially families, are moving to the Granite State. Who can blame them? They want to enjoy an enhanced quality of life.

Library Time

Peterborough established the nation's first tax-supported library in 1833. Today, the Granite State has 229 public libraries. ■

Granite State Firsts

Though it is a tiny state, New Hampshire has always been a leader. Here is a list of "firsts" achieved by the state over the years:

1719 First potato planted in the United States, at Londonderry by Scotch-Irish farmers.

1776 First colony with a written constitution.

1778 First state to hold a constitutional convention.

1833 First public library in the United States, established at Peterborough.

1849 First general library law, a law that allowed towns to use tax money to create public libraries.

1869 First cog railway able to climb steep grades, at Mount Washington.

1947 First use of artificial rain to fight a forest fire; scientists dropped dry ice over clouds to produce rain.

1952 Began the first-in-the-nation primary election.

1964 First state lottery to finance schools; also first state lottery in the twentieth century.

Other states have since followed. ■

CHAPTER TEN

Arts, Entertainment, and the Good Life

Two roads diverged in a wood, and I—
I took the one less traveled by,
And that has made all the difference.
—Robert Frost (1874–1963)

The road taken by the poet Robert Frost led him to New Hampshire. Frost was born in California but wrote some of his most powerful poems while living in the town of Derry. Over the years, New Hampshire has been the workplace—and the birthplace—of many other great artists, writers, and composers.

The Written Word

Horace Greeley (1811–1872) was born in Amherst, New Hampshire. At an early age, he moved to New York City, where he founded the *New York Tribune*. In one famous line, "Go West, young man," Greeley transformed life in the United States. He advised enterprising people in New York and New England to emigrate to the raw lands beyond the Mississippi River, and millions followed his recommendation. Thomas Bailey Aldrich (1836–1907) was born in Portsmouth and moved to Boston, where he became an editor of the *Atlantic Monthly* magazine. He reflected on his New Hampshire youth in two popular books: *Story of a Bad Boy* and *An Old Town by the Sea*.

Poet Robert Frost lived in Derry for a time.

Opposite: The Saint-Gaudens National Historic Site

After leaving his home in New Hampshire, Horace Greeley founded the *New York Tribune*.

The poet John Greenleaf Whittier (1807–1892) spent many summers in New Hampshire. His poems fell into two categories: those that attacked slavery and those that sang the praises of nature. In New Hampshire, he concentrated on the trees, the lakes, and the wonderful scenery that surrounded him.

The White Mountain town of Franconia was a refuge for famous literary figures such as Washington Irving (1783–1859), Henry Wadsworth Longfellow (1807–1882), and Nathaniel Hawthorne (1804–1864). Franconia is only 6 miles (10 km) from the Old Man of the Mountain, the face on a cliff that symbolizes New Hampshire. In his story "The Great Stone Face," Nathaniel Hawthorne wrote, "It was a happy lot for children to grow up to manhood or womanhood with the Great Stone Face before their eyes, for all the features were noble, and the expression was at once grand and sweet, as if it were the glow of a vast, warm heart that embraced all mankind in its affections, and had room for more."

A writers' colony developed in the late 1800s on the Isles of Shoals. Writer and poet Celia Laighton Thaxter (1835–1894) sponsored the colony. Thaxter's father was a lighthouse keeper on the White Island, one of the Isles of Shoals. Growing up on an island was a lonely experience, so Celia turned to writing to combat boredom. Among her writings was a tense mystery story called "A Memorable Murder," which was set on the islands. Thaxter later invited literary friends including Longfellow, Whittier, Emerson, and Harriet Beecher Stowe (author of *Uncle Tom's Cabin*) to live with her in a splendid 300-room hotel that was built on Appledore Island.

A Famous but Little Known Poet

Sarah Josepha Hale (1788–1879) was born on a farm near the New Hampshire town of Newport. She was a poet, a writer, and a magazine editor, and she had close friends in government. In the 1860s, she persuaded President Abraham Lincoln to declare Thanksgiving a national holiday. Every American child learns the lines of one of her poems, but few people—children or adults—know much about the author. In 1830, Sarah Josepha Hale wrote "Mary Had a Little Lamb..." ■

The beloved American humorist Mark Twain (1835–1910) had a summer home in Dublin. Willa Cather (1873–1947), who wrote stirring novels about pioneer women, spent her summers in Jaffrey. Louisa May Alcott (1832–1888), creator of the classic novel *Little Women,* lived in the town of Walpole on the Connecticut River.

New Hampshire continues to contribute to U.S. literature. Donald Hall (1928–) lives in Wilmot and is the state poet laureate. In addition to being an outstanding poet, Hall writes books for young readers. J. D. Salinger (1919–) is the author of the 1951 novel *The Catcher in the Rye*, a book adored by high school and college students. Salinger lives in Cornish. John Irving—born in 1942 in Exeter—is the author of many best-sellers including the novel *The World According to Garp* (1978).

J. D. Salinger (above) is best known for writing *The Catcher in the Rye.*

Novelist John Irving (left) was born in Exeter.

The Colonial Theater in Keene

The town of Keene is proud of its Colonial Theater, an organization that has been putting on productions for more than seventy-five years. The theater building on Main Street presents plays and other events ranging from classic movies to Mozart operas. ■

Granite State Arts and Crafts

The Saint-Gaudens National Historic Site, near Cornish, was once home to a famous artists' colony. The Irish-born sculptor Augustus Saint-Gaudens (1848–1907) came to Cornish in 1885. One of his greatest works was a stunning statue of Abraham Lincoln, which still stands in Chicago's Lincoln Park. In Cornish, Saint-Gaudens gathered around him some of the finest artists of his day—the illustrator Maxfield Parrish, the portrait painter Kenyon Cox, and others. Visitors tour the colony and recall the time when it blossomed with artistic genius. Another creator of public art was Daniel Chester French (1850–1931), who was born in Exeter.

French fashioned the most famous Lincoln statue of all, the seated Lincoln that graces the Lincoln Memorial in Washington, D.C.

Major art galleries in New Hampshire include the Currier Gallery of Art in Manchester, the Dartmouth College Museum and Galleries at Hanover, the University Art Galleries in Durham, and the Lamont Gallery in Exeter. In those galleries, visitors see paintings and sculptures by masters from around the world. But art in New Hampshire is not confined to museums. Three hundred years of folk art, crafts, and architecture can be enjoyed in every part of this state.

The creation of handmade crafts is an old New Hampshire tradition. Such crafts range from weavings to wood carvings. One place to shop for these items is at the New Hampshire Homecraft Cooperative in Campton. The cooperative's shop is in a very interesting one-room schoolhouse built in 1878. The League of New Hampshire Craftsmen in Concord hosts an annual fair at Sunapee State Park during the first week in August.

Sculptor Daniel Chester French

Stone Walls: A Yankee Art Form

In the 1800s, Yankee farmers in the New Hampshire hill country cursed the huge stones and boulders they found in their fields. But "waste not, want not" was an old Yankee saying. Painstakingly, the farmers moved the stones from their fields and used them to make fences. They were difficult to build since a farmer had to puzzle together a wall out of one stone shaped like a thick pancake and another shaped like a football. Yet the fences went up. Some claimed they had a pleasing, even artistic appearance. The stone walls still stand, often on land that was abandoned years ago and is now overgrown with tall trees. ■

Peterborough, City of the Arts

Few small cities anywhere in the country can boast a livelier art scene than Peterborough. All the arts are represented in this village of about 6,000 people. Peterborough is home to the MacDowell Colony, training ground of writers and musicians. The Monadnock Music Chamber Orchestra performs here. Children love the New England Marionettes, a local group that performs opera with puppets. The Peterborough Players present plays in a theater converted from an eighteenth-century barn. Truly, art is king in Peterborough. ■

New Hampshire architecture is a blending of history and the builders' craft. The Strawbery Banke neighborhood of Portsmouth is one of the most visited spots in New Hampshire. Spreading over 10 acres (4 ha), many Strawbery Banke houses are older than the nation itself. The Barrett House in Ipswich, built in 1800, attracts visitors interested in history as well as in architecture. A spectacular mansion called the Castle in the Clouds was built near Center Harbor in 1911. A millionaire named Thomas Plant employed as many as 1,000 workers to construct the Castle in the Clouds, which is now open to the public.

Visitors flock to New Hampshire to tour its famous covered bridges. Some bridges are more than 150 years old. The slanting roofs built over the bridges protect them in winter by forcing snow to slide off, thus preventing snow buildup, which could weaken the structure. Ironically, road workers in the old days had to shovel snow *inside* the bridges to allow the passage of horse-drawn sleds. There are more than fifty covered bridges in New Hampshire. The bridge spanning the Connecticut River at Cornish, built in 1866, is 460 feet (140 m) long, making it the longest covered bridge in the United States.

The Sporting Life

No major professional sports teams play in New Hampshire. State residents generally follow the teams from Boston, such as the Red Sox baseball team and the New England Patriots football team. Dartmouth and the University of New Hampshire have sports teams, but they generate little interest outside the state. So, with no big-time teams to cheer for, New Hampshirites become participants in sports rather than mere spectators.

The entire outdoors is New Hampshire's gymnasium. Approximately 6,000 miles (9,654 km) of hiking trails lace the state. A popular trek is the 230-mile (370-km) New Hampshire Heritage

This covered bridge in Cornish is the longest in the United States.

Canoeing on Echo Lake

Trail. The trail begins at the Canadian border, winds through the mountain towns of Colebrook, Lancaster, and Franconia Notch, and ends far to the south in Nashua. Many rugged hikers walk the entire length of the New Hampshire Heritage Trail, camping along the way.

Camping, hiking, and boating are major summertime activities. A state pamphlet claims, "There are so many wonderful trails in New Hampshire that you could be a hiker for a lifetime and not hike them all." Try the three-hour, 2.5 mile (4-km) Sanguinari Trail, which starts at Dixville Notch and offers a spectacular view of Lake Gloriette. Dozens of campgrounds and RV (recreation vehicle) parks are scattered throughout the state. Camping is such a popular activity that it is advisable to call ahead for reservations. Boating, canoeing, and kayaking are fun on New Hampshire's endless lakes and rivers.

Mountain climbing and rock climbing provide breathtaking thrills, but they are not for the untrained. Mount Washington has been called the most dangerous small mountain in the world. Sudden temperature drops and wind gusts can turn Mount Washington's trails into treacherous paths. Nearby is a steep rock called Cannon Cliff. Four rock climbers have been killed trying to scale the stark and often frozen face of Cannon

Rock climbing is a sport that requires experience and skill.

Climb the Monadnock

Mount Monadnock, at 3,165 feet (965 m), is not tall as mountains go, but it can be seen for miles because it rises in the relatively flat lands of southwestern New Hampshire. It is also a gentle mountain, with dozens of hiking trails. State officials claim Monadnock is the second-most-climbed mountain in the world after Mount Fuji in Japan. ■

Cliff. Experts should accompany beginners when trekking over the tough peaks of the Granite State.

More than eighty golf courses are open to the public in New Hampshire. *Golf Magazine* recently hailed the Balsams Grand Resort Hotel near Dixville Notch as "One of America's best golf resorts." Tennis courts and neighborhood basketball courts are busy in the summers and even when the weather gets chilly.

One of the state's many impressive golf courses

New Hampshire is the perfect state for a winter holiday. Snow-covered peaks in the White Mountains offer alpine or cross-country skiing. The state has twenty-one alpine ski resorts and twenty-four Nordic centers. Other winter activities abound—snowmobiling, snowshoeing, snow-tubing, ice fishing, and winter hiking. In this state, people refuse to hibernate. They get out and enjoy winter sports.

Summer and winter sports are a few of the many activities offered by the Granite State. New Hampshire is an exciting place to visit and a proud place to live. It is a different state: friendly, beautiful, prosperous, and above all—independent.

Timeline

United States History

1607 The first permanent English settlement is established in North America at Jamestown.

1620 Pilgrims found Plymouth Colony, the second permanent English settlement.

1776 America declares its independence from Britain.

1783 The Treaty of Paris officially ends the Revolutionary War in America.

1787 The U.S. Constitution is written.

1803 The Louisiana Purchase almost doubles the size of the United States.

1812–15 The United States and Britain fight the War of 1812.

New Hampshire State History

1603 Martin Pring explores the mouth of the Piscataqua River.

1614 John Smith arrives in New Hampshire.

1622 Captain John Mason and Sir Ferdinando Gorges receive a large land grant that includes present-day New Hampshire.

1641 The Massachusetts Colony gains control of New Hampshire.

1679 New Hampshire becomes a separate royal colony.

1774 The first act of rebellion against the British occurs when rebels seize the fort at New Castle.

1776 New Hampshire declares independence from Britain.

1788 New Hampshire becomes the ninth state in the Union on June 21.

1808 The state capitol is established in Concord.

United States History

The North and South fight **1861–65** each other in the American Civil War.

The United States is **1917–18** involved in World War I.

The stock market crashes, **1929** plunging the United States into the Great Depression.

The United States **1941–45** fights in World War II.

The United States becomes a **1945** charter member of the U.N.

The United States **1951–53** fights in the Korean War.

The U.S. Congress enacts a series of **1964** groundbreaking civil rights laws.

The United States **1964–73** engages in the Vietnam War.

The United States and other **1991** nations fight the brief Persian Gulf War against Iraq.

New Hampshire State History

1853 Franklin Pierce of Hillsboro becomes president of the United States.

1911 The White Mountains National Forest is created.

1936 The Amoskeag textile mill complex closes.

1944 The International Monetary Conference is held at Bretton Woods.

1952 New Hampshire establishes its first-in-the-nation presidential primary.

1964 The New Hampshire sweepstakes lottery begins (the first legal lottery in the United States since the 1890s).

1986 Christa McAuliffe of Concord dies in the space shuttle *Challenger* disaster.

1996 Jeanne Shaheen is elected the first woman governor of New Hampshire.

Fast Facts

State capitol

Statehood date	June 21, 1788; the ninth state
Origin of state name	Named in 1629 by Captain John Mason of Plymouth Council for his home county in England
State capital	Concord
State nickname	Granite State
State motto	"Live Free or Die"
State animal	White-tailed deer
State bird	Purple finch
State flower	Purple lilac
State insect	Ladybug

Red-spotted newt

State amphibian	Red-spotted newt
State butterfly	Karner blue
State saltwater fish	Striped bass
State freshwater fish	Brook trout
State rock	Granite
State mineral	Bery
State gem	Smoky quartz
State song	"Old New Hampshire"
State tree	White birch
State wildflower	Pink lady's slipper
Total area; rank	9,283 sq. mi. (24,043 sq km); 44th
Land; rank	8,969 sq. mi. (23,230 sq km); 44th
Water; rank	314 sq. mi. (813 sq km); 46th
Inland water; **rank**	314 sq. mi. (813 sq km); 43rd
Geographic center	Belknap, 3 miles (5 km) east of Ashland
Latitude and longitude	New Hampshire is located approximately between 42° 40' and 45° 18' N and 70° 37' and 72° 37' W
Highest point	Mount Washington, 6,288 feet (1,918 m)
Lowest point	Sea level at the Atlantic Ocean
Largest city	Manchester
Number of counties	10
Population; rank	1,113,915 (1990 census); 41st
Density	120 persons per sq. mi. (46 per sq km)

Mount Washington

Fishing in New Hampshire

Population distribution 51% urban, 49% rural

Ethnic distribution (does not equal 100%)

White	98.03%
Hispanic	1.02%
Asian and Pacific Islanders	0.84%
African-American	0.65%
Native American	0.19%
Other	0.28%

Record high temperature 106°F (41°C) at Nashua on July 4, 1911

Record low temperature −46°F (−43°C) at Pittsburg on January 28, 1925

Average July temperature 68°F (20°C)

Average January temperature 19°F (−7°C)

Average annual precipitation 42 inches (107 cm)

Natural Areas and Historic Sites

National Scenic Trail
Appalachian National Scenic Trail is a 2,158-mile (3,473-km) trail extending the length of the Appalachian Mountains from Maine to Georgia.

National Historic Site
Saint-Gaudens National Historic Site preserves the home, studio, and gardens of sculptor Augustus Saint-Gaudens.

White Mountains National Forest

National Forests

White Mountains National Forest covers 769,147 acres (311,505 ha) of northeastern New Hampshire. Its forests are hardwood and it contains the largest alpine region east of the Rocky Mountains and south of Canada.

State Parks

New Hampshire maintains 42 state parks.

Sports Teams

NCAA Teams (Division 1)

Darmouth College Big Green
University of New Hampshire Wildcats

Cultural Institutions

Libraries

Baker Library at Dartmouth University (Hanover) contains an impressive collection of original manuscripts by such writers as Joseph Conrad, Robert Burns, and Herman Melville.

Museums

The Currier Gallery of Art (Manchester) holds the state's finest collection of paintings, including many notable works by important U.S. and European artists.

The Museum of New Hampshire History (Concord) contains important collections related to the state's history.

The Hood Museum of Art at Dartmouth (Hanover) also has a fine collection of art.

The New Hampshire Historical Society (Concord) contains interesting period rooms and collections of materials related to the state's history.

The Currier Gallery of Art

The University of
New Hampshire

Performing Arts

New Hampshire has one major opera company.

Universities and Colleges

In the late 1990s, New Hampshire had 12 public and 18 private institutions of higher learning.

Annual Events

January–March

Winter Carnivals in Franconia, Hanover, Lincoln, and Plymouth (January and February)

Annual World Championship Sled Dog Derby in Laconia (February)

April–June

All-State Music Festival (April)

Sheep and Wool Festival in New Boston (May)

Stark Fiddler's Contest (June)

Market Square Days Celebration in Portsmouth (mid-June)

July–September

Prescott Parks Art Festival in Portsmouth (July and August)

Pemi Valley Bluegrass Festival in Campton (August)

League of New Hampshire Craftsmen's Fair in Mount Sunapee State Park (August)

Riverfest Celebration in Manchester (September)

Highland Games at Mount Loon in Lincoln (September)

October–December

Fall Foliage Tour in Charlestown (October)

Sandwich Fair (October)

Candlelight Stroll at Strawbery Banke in Portsmouth (December)

First Night New Hampshire in Concord, Keene, Portsmouth, and Wolfeboro (December 31)

**Sarah Josepha
Buell Hale**

Famous People

Lewis Cass (1782–1866)	Public official
Salmon Portland Chase (1808–1873)	Chief justice of the U.S. Supreme Court
Jonas Chickering (1798–1853)	Piano manufacturer
Ralph Adams Cram (1863–1942)	Architect
John Adams Dix (1798–1879)	Soldier, public official
Mary Morse Baker Eddy (1821–1910)	Religious leader
Sam Walter Foss (1858–1911)	Poet and journalist
Daniel Chester French (1850–1931)	Sculptor
Horace Greeley (1811–1872)	Journalist and political leader
John Parker Hale(1806–1873)	Public official
Sarah Josepha Buell Hale (1788–1879)	Editor and author
John Irving (1942–)	Author
Thaddeus Sobieski Coulincout Lowe (1832–1913)	Balloonist and inventor
Franklin Pierce (1804–1869)	U.S. president
John Stark (1728–1822)	Revolutionary soldier
John Sullivan (1740–1795)	Revolutionary soldier and public official
Daniel Webster (1782–1852)	Lawyer and public official
Benning Wentworth (1696–1770)	Merchant and public official
John (Long John) Wentworth (1737–1820)	Editor and public official
Paul Wentworth (?–1793)	U.S. vice president

John Irving

To Find Out More

History

- Brown, Dottie. *New Hampshire*. Minneapolis: Lerner Publications Company, 1993.

- Fradin, Dennis Brindell. *New Hampshire*. Chicago: Childrens Press, 1992.

- Fradin, Dennis Brindell. *The New Hampshire Colony*. Chicago: Childrens Press, 1992.

- Thompson, Kathleen. *New Hampshire*. Austin, Tex.: Raintree/Steck Vaughn, 1996.

Biography

- Bober, Natalie S. *A Restless Spirit: The Story of Robert Frost*. New York: Henry Holt, 1998.

- Graves, Charles Parlin. *John Smith*. New York: Chelsea House, 1991.

Fiction

- Blos, Joan W. *A Gathering of Days: A New England Girl's Journal, 1830–32*. New York: Atheneum, 1980.

- Bruchac, Joseph. *Heart of a Chief: A Novel*. New York: Dial Books for Young Readers, 1998.

- Curry, Jane Louise. *Moon Window*. New York: Margaret McElderry, 1996.

Websites

- **Webster: New Hampshire State Government Online**
  http://www.state.nh.us/
  The official website of the state of New Hampshire

- **New Hampshire Office of Travel and Tourism Development**
  http://www.visitnh.gov/
  Offers information about New Hampshire's many travel destinations and the state's geography

- **White Mountains National Forest**
  http://www.fs.fed.us/r9/white/
  Provides information on the forest's conservation plan, recreation facilities, and links to other sites of interest

Addresses

- **New Hampshire Office of Travel and Tourism Development**
  172 Pembroke Road
  P.O. Box 1856
  Concord, NH 03302
  For information about travel and tourism in New Hampshire

- **Department of Resources and Economic Development**
  172 Pembroke Road
  P.O. Box 1856
  Concord, NH 03302
  For information about New Hampshire's economy

- **Office of Citizen Services**
  Governor's Office
  State House
  Concord, NH 03301
  For information about New Hampshire's government

- **New Hampshire State Library**
  Bureau of Reference and Loan
  20 Park Street
  Concord, NH 03301
  For information about New Hampshire's history

Index

Page numbers in *italics* indicate illustrations.

Meet the Author

I'm R. Conrad Stein, and I write books for young readers. Over the years, I've published more than 100 books aimed at a young audience. I was born and grew up in Chicago. At age eighteen, I enlisted in the Marines. Later I graduated from the University of Illinois with a degree in history. I now live in Chicago with my wife, Deborah Kent (who is also an author of books for young readers), and our daughter, Janna.

I very much enjoy my writing projects. Although I write mainly history and geography books, I try to present them in story form so that they are more interesting for the readers. My job also allows me to travel to the places I write about. I have been to almost all the fifty states and to many foreign countries. Traveling is a hobby to me. I look upon my journeys as an education as well as a pleasure. To prepare for this book I took a long trip up and down New Hampshire. As a lifelong traveler, I attest that the Granite State is one of the most beautiful places I have ever seen.

Photo Credits

Photographs ©:

AP/Wide World Photos: 84 (Jim Cole), 89 (John Mottern)

Archive Photos: 97 top (Consolidated News), 97 bottom (George Dabrowsky), 33 (R. Gates), 111 top, 31, 37 (Kean Collection), 118 (Museum of the City of New York), 23, 29, 47, 119 top, 119 center, 121, 135 top

Bob LaPree Photography: 16, 65, 85, 90, 93 top, 96, 99

Bruce Iverson: 45, 71, 101 top, 104 top, 111 bottom, 113

Corbis-Bettmann: 119 bottom, 135 bottom (Marko Shark)

Courtesy of Claremont Opera House: 77

Envision: 103 (Steven Needham)

Kindra Clineff: 7 bottom, 40, 57, 69, 104 bottom, 116

Liaison Agency, Inc.: 117 (Hulton Getty), 114, 134 (James H. Pickerell), 6 top center, 55, 126 top (Brian Smith)

Martin A. Levick: 50

Michael Moore: 120

Museum of New Hampshire History: 13, 15

NASA: 48

New England Stock Photo: 7 top right, 60, 98, 106, 110, 132 (Brooks Dodge), back cover (Richard Durnan), 6 top right, 7 top center, 11, 49, 101 bottom (William Johnson), 62 (Bill Lea), 9 (Thomas H. Mitchell), cover (L. O'Shaughnessy), 73, 75, 82, 83, 109, 130 (Jim Schwabel), 42, 133 top (Kevin Shields), 126 bottom (Frank Siteman)

New Hampshire Farm Museum: 78

New Hampshire Historical Society, Concord, NH: 19, 20, 24, 35 top, 39

New Hampshire Travel & Tourism: 56 (Nancy G. Horton/Courtesy State of New Hampsire), 124 (Dennis Welsh), 7 top left, 125

North Wind Picture Archives: 6 bottom, 12, 14, 17, 28, 32, 38, 41

Photo Researchers: 66 (Garry McMichael), 59 (Lawrence Migdale), 61 (George Ranalli), 76 (Joe Sohm/Chromosohm)

Stock Montage, Inc.: 35 bottom, 43

Superstock, Inc.: 105 (John W. Warden), 63, 72, 80, 133 bottom

The Image Works: 26 (Stuart Cohen), 6 top left, 58 (Jenny Hager), 22, 25, 123 (Lee Snider), 52, 131 bottom (J. Sohm/Chromosohm), 2 (Topham)

Tony Stone Images: 36, 67 (Doris De Witt), 53 (Joseph Sohm)

Visuals Unlimited: 30 (A. Corton), 92 (Barbara Gerlach), 102 (Ned Therrien), 8 (Roger Treadwell), 93 bottom, 131 top (William J. Weber)

Woodfin Camp & Associates: 107 (Paula Lerner)

Maps by XNR Productions, Inc.